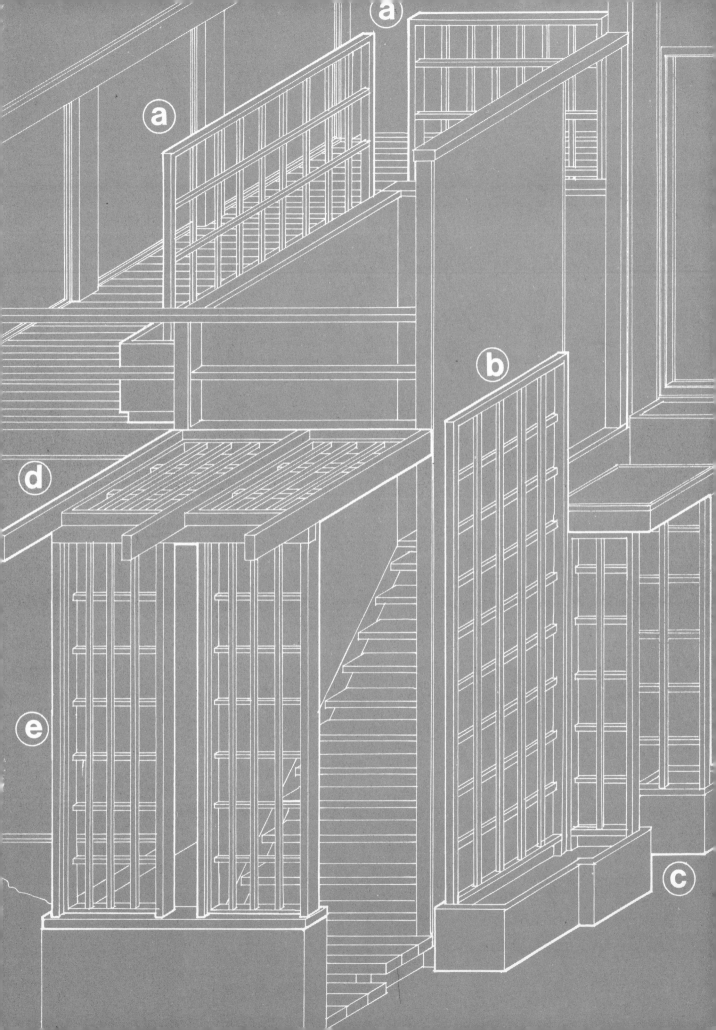

your trellis garden

how to build it
how to grow it
how to show it

by Jack Kramer

Drawings by Michael G. Valdez

WALKER AND COMPANY

NEW YORK

Insert Photos by Jerry Bagger, Matthew Barr
Cover Photo by Max Erkert

First published in the United States of America in
1976 by the Walker Publishing Company, Inc.
Published simultaneously in Canada by Fitzhenry &
Whiteside, Limited, Toronto
ISBN: 0-8027-0532-4
Library of Congress Catalog Card Number:
75-43989
Lithographed in the United States of America
under the supervision of
Rolls Offset Printing Co., Inc., N.Y.

10   9   8   7   6   5   4   3   2   1

Contents

Introduction

A framework of crossed wood strips, trellis (or lattice), is so versatile that it can be used as a support for plants or by itself as decorative accent. You can frame windows, create screens to emphasize a scene, or use trellises as a sun shield against large expanses of glass *(this not only breaks the sun's rays but also establishes eye interest in an otherwise monotonous wall of glass)*. You can use trellises to screen unsightly areas like basements or garbage can areas.

Trelliswork or latticework *(and the words are used interchangeably in this book),* is really an old garden art. In some countries, primarily Britain, trellis was first used as a wall or fence. The old-fashioned summerhouse was generally a trellis that supported climbing plants and fruit trees. The framework of the trellis was made of everyday timber and elms, limes, and other trees were the plants trained to the trellis. Trellises were also used as arbors, open-closed parts of the garden where herbs were grown. Eventually, the trellised arbor evolved into a tunnel with plants; a cloistered and shady retreat and by the sixteenth century, the tunnel-type trellis was considered a necessary part of a really fine garden. Towards the end of the sixteenth century, the French created highly elaborate structures called *trelliages;* the word denotes a more refined and architectural use of trellises.

In the eighteenth century, French-inspired trellis work was immensely popular in Britain and English books recommended that trellises be made of fine oak strips. Trelliswork became the accent of many gardens, some elaborately constructed and highly attractive.

The trellis was a very important part of yesteryear's gardens, both decorative and useful *(to support plants)*. And today the trellis can be as useful as it was years ago – more so – to save space and to provide a garden, as well as add charm to today's buildings and property.

**For pure decorative effect it is hard to beat this gazebo type entrance.
The trellis is used for pattern and drama.** *(Photo by Max Eckert).*

1 Advantages of Trellis Gardening

Beautiful gardens, whether decorative or productive, are not only for people with lots of land. There is a way to provide beauty and profit in very little space; it's called trellis gardening, which is vertical rather than the traditional horizontal gardening. To garden in the air, some kind of supports for plants are necessary, namely, trellises, *(sometimes called lattices)*. These wooden structures are decorative as well as functional. Vegetables like squash and cucumbers can be grown on trellises, fruit trees can be espaliered on the supports for maximum growing, and berries do very well on trellises. And don't forget attractive vines such as clematis and bougainvillea which can add superlative spring and summer color outdoors.

The advantages of a trellis garden are many, but perhaps the most important one is that you can grow a lot in a little space, and with land at a premium these days, this is a prime consideration.

Minimum Space Gardening

Trellis gardening requires no more space than what a few planter boxes filled with soil need: an area about 8 feet long by 2 feet wide. By growing plants vertically you increase growing space several times that involved with horizontal ground gardening. Even a back porch or a small entryway becomes a verdant greenery when trellises are installed.

If your outdoor area is a patio, you may want a decorative effect; arbors and trellises adorned with plants add charm to any area. If the space is a doorway, grow some vegetables. Or if somewhat larger, grow some fruit trees against trellis structures. By extending the trellis work with an overhead canopy, you can create a beautiful hanging garden of vines *(grapes, for example)*.

You can use trellises as fences, walls, screens, canopies, arbors, pergolas, and gazebos. There are numerous places to create your trellis garden; so why not enjoy the delights of vertical gardening?

Letting Trellises Work for You

I said that growing plants on trellises lets you grow more in little space. This is quite true, but there are even more reasons to consider trellis gardening. If you are advancing into the middle years or actually into the middle years, it is very good sense to garden intelligently, that is, without undue effort. Stooping and bending are fine exercises to a point, but too much is too much. It is much easier to walk around your garden and tend plants at waist and eye level than it is to have to lie or stoop on the ground. Also, you can see better in a standing position than looking at plants from a distance.

Trellis gardening thus affords you a less strenuous way to gar-

9

den, and it also helps the plant. Air reaches all parts of the plant and when plants have a good circulation of air around them, they grow better. If I have not yet convinced you that trellis gardening is *the* way to garden, let me add that growing plants vertically eliminates many insects simply because insects do not like to crawl any more than you do; if there is horizontal fodder on your neighbor's land, they will migrate to that rather than risk the long climb to your plants.

Easy Installation

If you look at old charming neighborhoods, you will see weatherworn trellises from years ago still standing and serving the gardener. If your property has some, you are fortunate, but if not, you can make trellises with very little carpentry knowledge; we tell you how in chapter 4. Once trellises are constructed, their installation is simple: secure them to the ground with posts or with stakes. The trellis can be built against a fence or wall, utilizing otherwise useless space, or it can be nailed to the planter box or staked in soil, depending on the situation. In any case, it is easy to install a trellis; it can be done in a day. Furthermore, a trellis you make is inexpensive and there is satisfaction of making something yourself.

Training plants like vegetables and vines to trellises requires some work at the start because plants have to be tied and trained. But once started and only with some tieing of stems at the bottom of the wood support, plants will usually

find their way on their own – most are equipped with grasping tendrils or discs – and grow luxuriantly. Then all they need is occasional training, that is, tying the stems with string or plastic tie-ons *(at suppliers)* to the wood members.

Decorative Effect

Besides the utilitarian features of trellis, there is aesthetics involved. There is little better way to increase the interest and charm of a garden whether small or large, than with decorative trellis work. The wood structure provides vertical eye interest in otherwise horizontal stretches of garden; this is an important aspect of good garden design; that is balancing the horizontal with the vertical lines. The primary role of trellises is of course to support plants, but aesthetics too mean a great deal to the overall beauty of the garden.

An inexpensive, homemade, well-built trellis is quite versatile, but it must be used correctly. In many cases it is not wise to use too many plants – a tangle of foliage and stem may result. It is much better to use a deft hand and create a light and graceful look. Here are six general suggestions when using trellises:

1. For small-growing plants with small leaves, closer trellising is necessary.

2. When spanning a distance, trellises should always be in sections, with posts at intervals, to supply needed vertical accent when one design is repeated for a long distance without a break.

3. Laths must always be arranged to give adequate support

for plants *(where used exclusively for plants);* laths must be close enough to permit small shoots being secured.

4. If you are training plants against a flat surface, (espalier) use a trellis pattern that has sufficient space, generally 4 to 6 inches. Although many patterns are available, the grid pattern works best for espaliers.

5. Where shade and seclusion is paramount, use a close-patterned trellis to create a visual dramatic look in the intimate nook.

6. If there is a valuable scene on the other side of the trellis, space strips far apart so the peek-through look is achieved. This is quite handsome.

Small areas can be efficiently used when you have a trellis garden; this trellis screen is for beans and tomatoes. The vegetables are in planter boxes. *(Photo by Jerry Bagger)*.

The land area was small in this backyard garden so a diamond pattern trellis was erected on the fence to grow vegetables. Small plants have been started at the base of the trellis and will eventually be trained to the support. *(Photo by author)*.

There is beauty in a well-made trellis and this fence and pergola afford some privacy and yet allows air and light to enter the garden. The grid pattern is effective and adds dimension to the scene and growing space for plants if necessary. *(Photo by Matthew Barr)*.

FREE STANDING TRELLIS

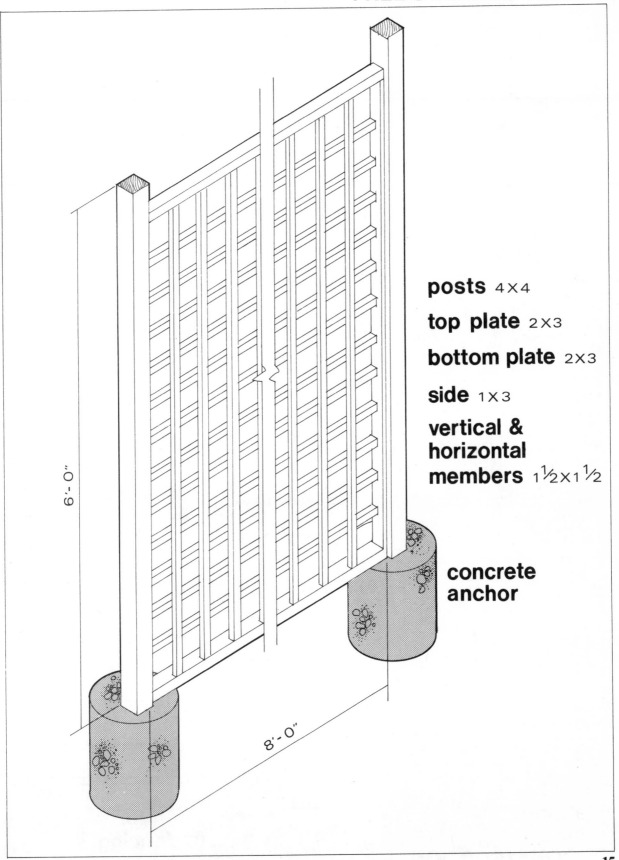

posts 4×4

top plate 2×3

bottom plate 2×3

side 1×3

vertical & horizontal members $1\frac{1}{2}$×$1\frac{1}{2}$

concrete anchor

6'-0"

8'-0"

TRELLIS AND PLANT SUPPORTS

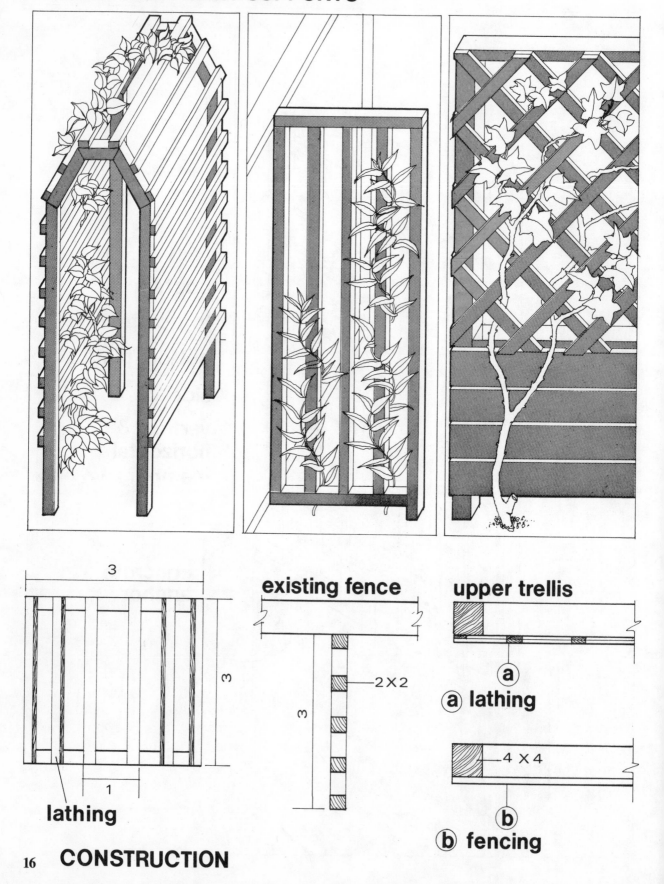

3

3

1

lathing

existing fence

2 × 2

3

upper trellis

(a)

(a) lathing

4 × 4

(b)

(b) fencing

CONSTRUCTION

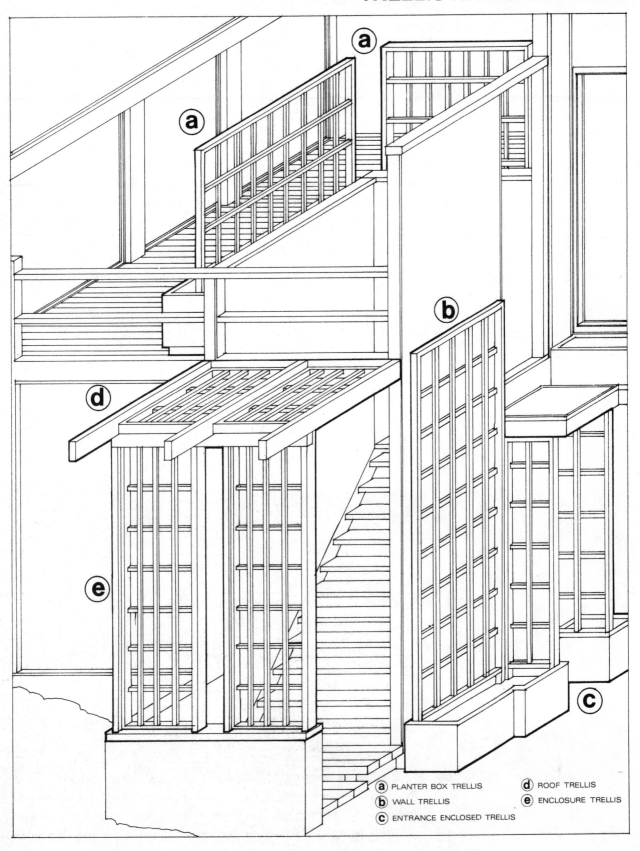

(a) PLANTER BOX TRELLIS   (d) ROOF TRELLIS

(b) WALL TRELLIS   (e) ENCLOSURE TRELLIS

(c) ENTRANCE ENCLOSED TRELLIS

Arbors provide infinite charm to a garden and this old-fashioned one is especially handsome festooned with wisteria. *(Photo by Matthew Barr).*

Even a simple commercial trellis *(at left)* **can act as a fence or screen and provide eye interest. It replaces a board fence which would shut out all light.** *(Photo by Matthew Barr).*

ⓐ coiling tendrils

GRAPE

ⓑ coiling leaf-stalk

CLEMATIS

ⓒ twining stems

STRING BEANS

ⓓ weaving stems

CLIMBING ROSE

Lattice gazebos have been part of yesteryears charm and can be equally effective in today's gardens. This one is beautifully made of redwood lath. *(Photo courtesy California Redwood Association).*

2 Trellis Placement

Trellises adapt to almost any outdoor area and enhance the property with good looks. In a yard they hide unsightly areas; on a patio they provide eye interest; and on a terrace, balcony or porch they create a dramatic effect. The vertical accent is highly important in all garden areas, and trellises supply drama.

Aside from growing plants on them, *(the primary use of trellises),* there are many ways to use these wood grids. Let us look at some specific situations and determine which type of trellis will work for you.

Yards

The yard is generally a small back area with some utility posts or other distracting features like garbage cans or neighbors' yards. Because of their space limitations, yards tend to be boxed-in areas. One side of the yard can have trellis work; a wall of trellis will act as a design element, eliminating the box look and serving as a fine place for plants, actually increasing the growing area four times. For example, if one side of the yard is 10 feet and you grow plants horizontally, you have 10 feet of growing area. But by installing trellises to a height of, say, 10 feet, you have 100 square feet of growing area!

Do not install too much trellis in a yard or you will create too much pattern in too little space, Cover one area: a screen, a divider, a fence. If the roof of a neighbor's house is near your fence, install trellis to the fence to camouflage the house. If the garbage-can area is in the yard, put a gazebo-type trellis structure around it and screen the trellis with plants to eliminate this unsightly area. If there are posts or other distracting structures in the background, build a triangular lattice, which will add accent and create additional growing space.

House Walls

Trellises are handsome on house walls or in entryways because they soften the severe architectural lines and provide colorful accents. The main problem with trellis-work on walls is that when it is time to paint the house, the plants must come down because the trellis and walls usually are painted at the same time. Even if the trellis is away from the wall *(as it should be),* there is almost no way to save plants. Still, most vining plants grow quickly; they can be replanted every few years. *(We discussed vines in Chapter 8.)*

For house walls and porch areas patterns should be simple; generally, vertical panels will supply the most pronounced statements, providing lovely color and eye interest. Another ideal place for house wall trellis is around windows and doorways, where it dresses up the house, providing a stunning effect.

Use heavy wood for wall and porch trellises; 1- x 1-inch stock is best because it is substantial and will last many years. Lathing is too rustic in appearance and too flimsy when used on walls.

The trellises against house walls can be staked into the ground, but it is better to use a frame construction for weight and durability.

Patios

The patio is the outdoor room, the place that is used more as a retreat from the house than as a place for growing plants. Trellises can add growing space to the paved area and provide the decorative accent so badly needed in patios. Most importantly, the grid pattern of trellis is exceptionally handsome with brick paving, and redwood, if used, is a natural complement to other patio materials.

For a delightful effect on the patio, use an L-shaped trellis structure in one corner; this defines the area and creates fine eye interest. If there are posts, consider boxing in the posts with four narrow panels of trellis to provide a charming picture.

If the paved area is concrete, use a more elaborate pattern of trellis – a starburst or geometrical design – to really brighten the area. A freestanding trellis itself will act as partial walls in the patio, bringing flair to the area and always causing guests to comment. No matter what pattern you decide to use, use it throughout the area; do not change patterns – diamond in one place, basket-weave in another – or you will create a spotty picture. It is important to keep the patio

area harmonious in all aspects. You can repeat the design of the trellis on the face of planters to create the total patio that is inviting to all.

Elaborate patios demand dramatic, painted trellises. White is especially pleasing, but pastel shades are also suitable.

Terraces and Balconies

Trellises are really tailor-made for terraces and balconies. These areas generally need definition, and simple fences or screens are not as handsome as a finely made trellis. The trellis structure in these areas is more than just a place for plants: it also buffers winds and provides a most effective privacy barrier, never obtrusive and always handsome.

On balconies, place trellises at each end or instead of the simple panels – one to a side – use an L-shaped structure, which eliminates the boxed-in look that a pair of screens can sometimes create.

On terraces, the trellis brings the warm feeling of wood to an area where most materials are masonry. For flair, use the more formal and decorative designs, such as sunbursts and geometric configurations.

Fences and Screens

The trellis can be overlaid on a fence or may be the fence itself. Solid-board fences are rarely handsome, but when you use a partial trellis and board fence, the effect can be stunning. Remember to

set the trellis in front of an existing fence; a good rule of thumb is 4 inches from the boards. Fence trellises, as most all trellises, should be constructed with suitable 4 x 4 posts and 2 x 4 railings as frames on which the trellis is nailed. A wobbly trellis is hardly a worthwhile investment.

Fence designs vary greatly for trellises, but basically the grid pattern is the best because it is never too dramatic or too busy. The handsome diamond pattern is frequently used too. More intricate patterns, with starbursts and sunbursts at the center of the fence, sometimes overburden the design and create too much drama.

Often a screen or divider area is needed in the garden or patio to define two separate areas, to create interest, or to guide traffic. A board fence can be used, but a free standing trellis screen is much more appealing. The screen can be of any length or height that is in keeping with the total design of the area: wider and higher screens for large sites, smaller, more intimate screens for the small site. Be sure that one end of the screen fits perpendicular to a house wall so it appears as part of the total landscape plan rather than as a tacked-on afterthought. Plants do not have to be used because often a decorative effect rather than an additional place for plants is what is wanted. Generally the trellis screen is painted and serves as "furniture."

Whether making trellis fences or screens, do a pencil sketch of the space available. Put in shapes of trees, shrubs, planters, and the fence or screen itself. You do not have to be an artist; even the crudest sketch will give you some idea of mass and volume, of balance and proportion, and that is what you are trying to achieve. It is much easier to erase on paper than to take down a trellis you built.

Arbors and Pergolas

Arbors are those delightful arched trellises usually overflowing with roses; so charming in any garden setting. Generally, the arbor replaces a gate, is an overhead structure where plants are grown, or is used just as a sun shade. The arbor by itself creates an additional small living area and defines the property.

The design and pattern of the arbor is vitally important; the arbor needs careful attention to proportion and design. A simple grid work pattern will not be effective as something more elaborate. You are creating a picture in this structure, so work out the design carefully, and use pleasing proportions.

A pergola is a structure that provides shade by means of plants over a terrace or path. It is really a handsome and lovely addition to a garden because it evokes memories of past days, when leisure walks were part of the daily life. Pergolas were often concrete or heavy-timbered long corridors, but today we see more of the lattice type because they are easy to make. Once a crude pole structure, the pergola can now be made in infinite designs.

The pergola cannot be just tacked on to a garden. It must have a definite purpose: It can extend the front or the rear walls of a house or delineate a terrace or a secluded section of the garden.

A vertical trellis with plants supplies needed vertical accent at the corner of the house; it creates just enough but not too much decoration to please the eye. *(Photo by Matthew Barr).*

23

The height depends on the space, the location or the arrangement of the buildings. Remember, you never want to cut the garden in two with a pergola; it should be a continuation at one end or the other of a terrace or patio area or an extension of the house. You can finish one end of the pergola walk with an arbor.

The pergola must be constructed with a strong framework. Proportions should be thought out ahead of time *(again, draw sketches)*. Allow enough headroom for a person to walk under, and also allow enough height for plants that may trail downward. It must be wide enough for two people to walk abreast.

Pergola posts should be 3 x 4s, placed at 16-inch centers to support the main framework; 2 x 4s can be used for the transverse beams above; on this framework nail the trellis pattern. Always put the posts in concrete because this must be a substantial structure. Lath is the best material for the skeleton of the pergola; finished wood such as 1/2 x 1/2 is not necessary because you want a rustic look rather than a furniture effect.

With the pergola you want decorative vines rather than vegetables or other, more utilitarian plants. Wisteria and grapes are perfect, but clematis is equally handsome, and passion flowers and any of the decorative vines

This small garden benefits greatly from trellis work; the handcrafted structure is very pleasing and adds beauty and plants. *(Photo by Matthew Barr)*.

mentioned in Chapter 8 are equally desirable.

Gazebos

These Victorian garden accompaniments are becoming more popular as pleasant retreats from the world. Gazebos are more difficult to build than any thing we have discussed, but as decorative additions to the outdoors they are most appealing.

I have been a fan of gazebos for years and consider them very worthwhile investments because they do provide the charm of yesterday. But more important, they create a retreat where you can watch the landscape. Generally, the location for the gazebo should be on slightly higher land rather than adjoining land. The gazebo is a place from which to look over, not look from. As an architectural structure, the gazebo will also be the accent of the garden and thus must be built with careful consideration as to materials and design. It must correlate with the main house and not be a tacked-on afterthought.

The gazebo is an open structure, and the application of trellis makes it a decorative one. There are gazebos without trelliege, but the really inviting ones always seem to have the added trellis work. Design of the trellis is vital, and some study is necessary to get with the right approach. You are dealing with a four- or six-sided structure with a roof; inside there is usually seating areas or benches. You do want a decorative structure, but nothing too overpowering. You want a distinctive design, so choose carefully.

This wall totally bare would hardly be pleasing; with the addition of simple trellis work, ivy vines create a handsome pattern. This is an easy installation that adds beauty to the total scene. *(Photo by Matthew Barr)*.

PORCH TRELLIS

front elevation

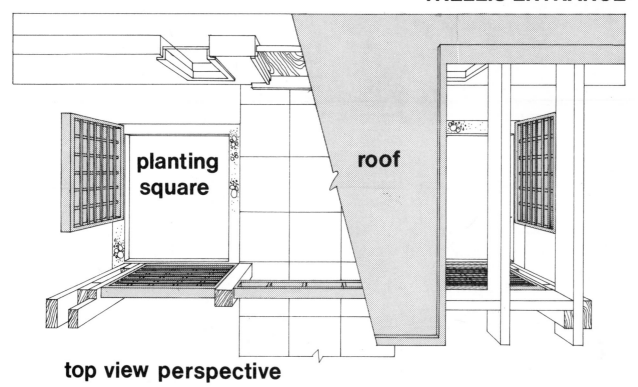

planting
square

roof

top view perspective

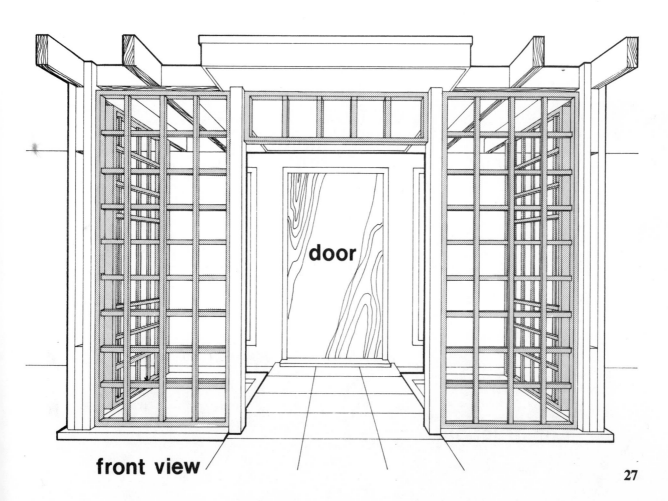

door

front view

PATIO TRELLIS

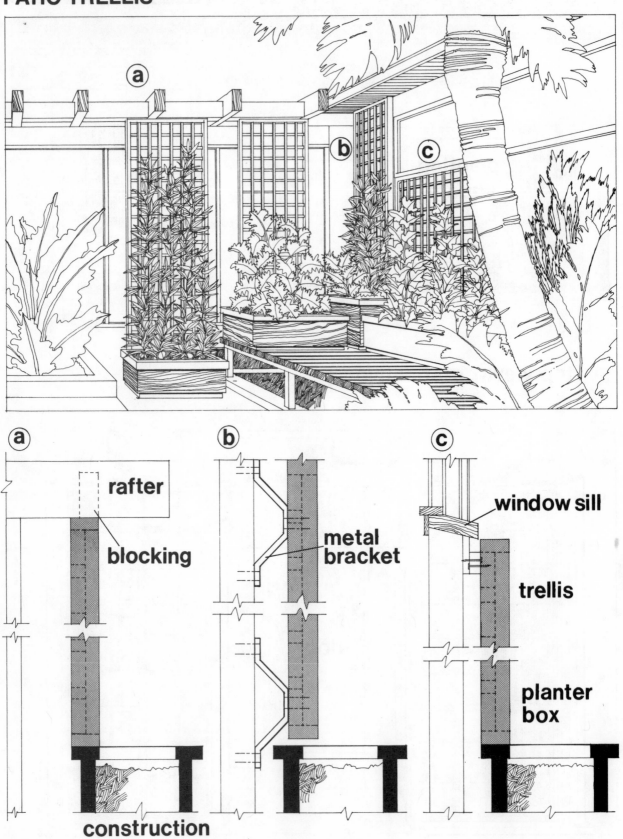

rafter

blocking

metal bracket

window sill

trellis

planter box

construction

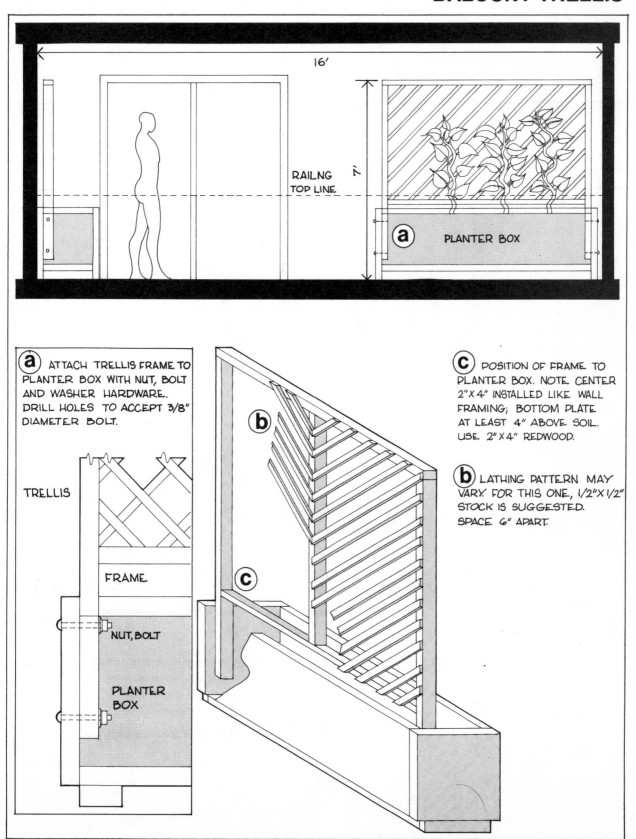

16'

7'

RAILNG TOP LINE

ⓐ PLANTER BOX

ⓐ ATTACH TRELLIS FRAME TO PLANTER BOX WITH NUT, BOLT AND WASHER HARDWARE. DRILL HOLES TO ACCEPT 3/8" DIAMETER BOLT.

TRELLIS

FRAME

NUT, BOLT

PLANTER BOX

ⓑ

ⓒ

ⓒ POSITION OF FRAME TO PLANTER BOX. NOTE CENTER 2"X 4" INSTALLED LIKE WALL FRAMING; BOTTOM PLATE AT LEAST 4" ABOVE SOIL. USE 2"X 4" REDWOOD.

ⓑ LATHING PATTERN MAY VARY. FOR THIS ONE, 1/2"X 1/2" STOCK IS SUGGESTED. SPACE 6" APART.

ARBOR TRELLIS

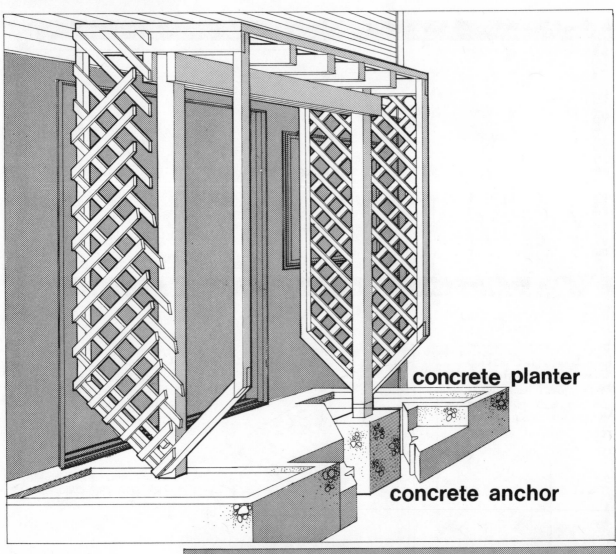

concrete planter

concrete anchor

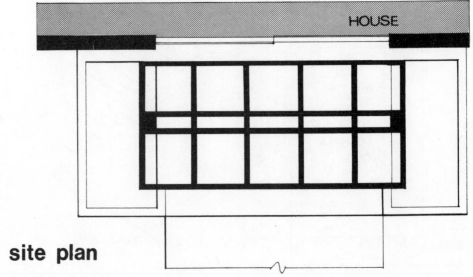

HOUSE

site plan

An ordinary balcony becomes an extraordinary one with handsome trellis ceiling and side panel. Plants are starting to grow on the ceiling trellis to provide silhouette and color. *(Photo by Matthew Barr)*.

Used as a screen near a doorway this hand made trellis is handsome and defines the space. *(Photo by Matthew Barr)*.

PERGOLA

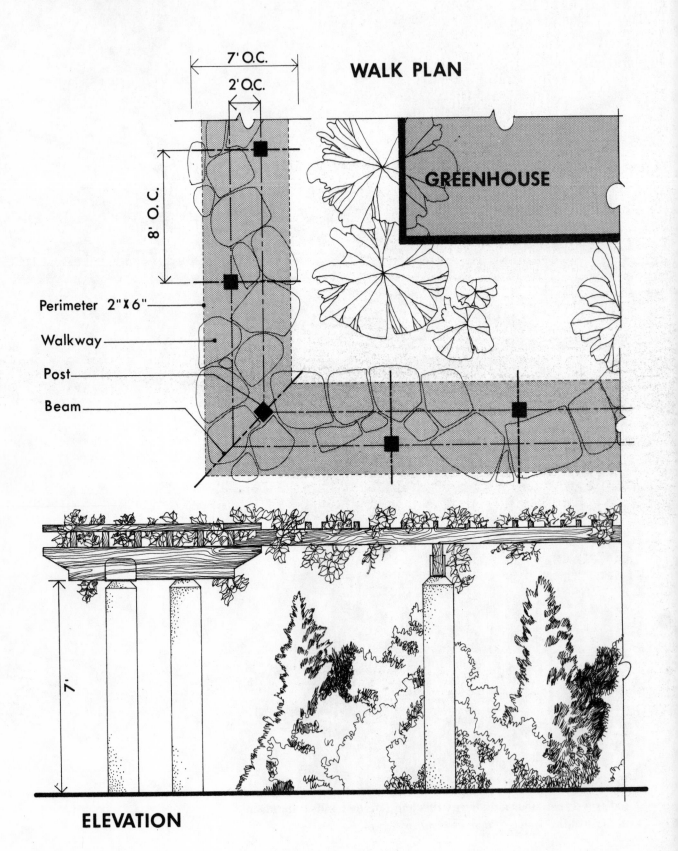

WALK PLAN

7' O.C.

2' O.C.

8' O.C.

GREENHOUSE

Perimeter 2"X6"

Walkway

Post

Beam

7'

ELEVATION

PERGOLA

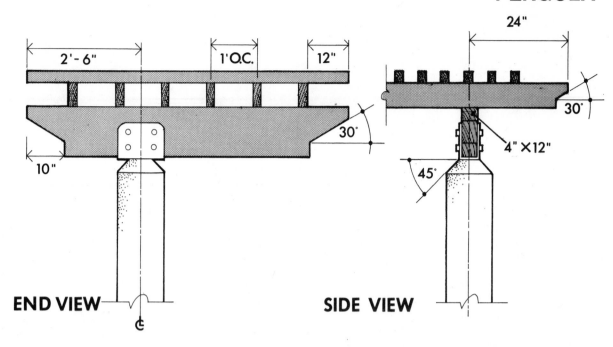

2'-6" **1' O.C.** **12"** **24"**

30° **10"** **4"×12"** **45°** **30°**

END VIEW **SIDE VIEW**

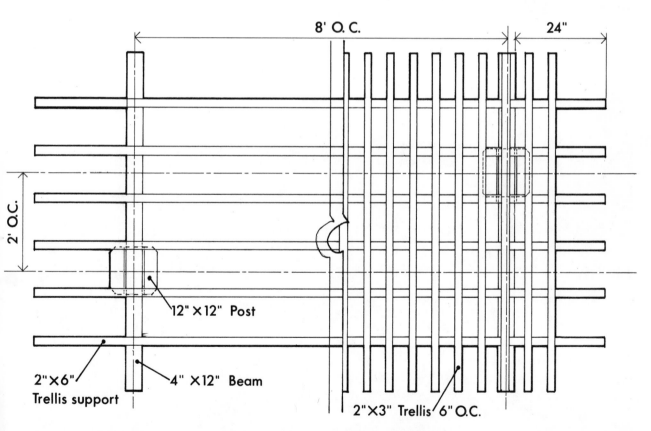

8' O.C. **24"**

2' O.C.

12"×12" Post

2"×6" Trellis support **4"×12" Beam**

2"×3" Trellis 6" O.C.

TOP VIEW

x

33

Acting as a fence, trellis with beans growing on it makes an effective barrier, both functional and useful; pretty too. *(Photo by Jerry Bagger).*

A grape arbor laden with foliage becomes a tunnel, the arbor long since hidden by the plant; yet, an effective and pleasing scene. *(Photo by author).*

3 What to Grow

In Chapter 1 we mentioned a few of the plants you can grow on trellises. Here we will discuss the many vining plants that can be grown vertically. As discussed, house and garage walls, fences, and various other flat areas are perfect for trellis gardening. Even if your garden is only 5 x 10 feet, you can grow a tremendous variety of plants for decoration and, in some cases, food.

Vegetables

Vegetables are discussed first because so many people with limited space think that they cannot grow them. But on trellises they can, and in fact the plants will fare better than if they were grown horizontally. For example, because squash and cucumbers are natural viners, they grow all over a garden, taking up space that could be perhaps used for a cutting garden. So let them grow up, not down, across, or sideways.

When you grow vegetables on trellises you also have the added advantage of the beauty of a green screen. The scalloped leaves of squash and cucumbers are handsome, and I am especially fond of green peppers on small trellis constructions. We have already discussed the advantages of trellis gardening, but perhaps most important (*considering today's produce costs*), is the fact that you can grow vegetables and fruits for nourishment. Peas, melons, cucumbers, apples, pears, and berries, whatever – you can enjoy the delightful taste of freshly grown, inexpensive harvest. (*Vegetables are fully discussed in Chapter 6.*)

Fruit Trees

Fruit trees bear bright flowers in early spring, have handsome, decorative foliage, and, like vegetables, produce free foods. Space is the problem that confronts most gardeners who want fruit trees, but even if space is limited, fruit trees can be grown flat against trellises in espalier style (*see Chapter 7*). Pear and apple trees adapt very well to trellis growing and are easier to tend than standard fruit trees because the fruit is at waist or eye level and is thus easy to harvest. And when grown against walls on trellises, fruit trees are protected from wind and get warmth from the wall covering.

There is some work in training the trees to the trellis, but it is not as hard as some books lead you to believe. In fact, I find working and training fruit trees in espalier fashion against trellises quite enjoyable because it is both an art and gardening. So do try the delights of growing your own fruit trees; you will be well rewarded.

Berries

Berries on trellises? Why not? It really is an excellent way of growing these plants. Blueberries, strawberries, and the like are easily grown on trellises, and to my way of thinking are easier to grow vertically than horizontally because they do not require the constant hacking necessary to keep them within bounds in the ground garden. Trellis gardening lets you grow a lot of berries in little space without sacrificing your garden. And in boxes with trellises you can train plants the way you want them and have a wealthy harvest. You need never be afraid that berries will take-over your garden.

As with vegetables and fruit trees, berries grown on trellises are easy to tend because they are at waist level and insects are not too much of a problem. Berry growing can be fun when you have plants on trellises; on the ground it can be a nuisance.

Decorative Vines

There is a world of good gardening sense when you grow decorative vines – both flowering and foliage types – on trellises and arbors. On trellises, vines can cover unsightly walls or be dividers, screens, or unequaled decorative accents that any gardener will be proud of *(we cover these fine plants in detail in Chapter 8)*. Vines also grow very fast, which is an excellent encouragement if you are an impatient gardener. A garden with vines is always more charming than any other kind of garden because there is always that natural feeling, so essential in good landscape planning.

If by now you have the idea that I like vines, I do. To me they are the finishing touch to a garden, and more importantly perhaps, it gives the average person a chance to grow not-so-average plants like clematis and passionflower. Vines open up a world of overlooked foliage and flowering gems.

The clinging tendrils of squash show how the vine grasps wooden trellises; it is one of the best plants for trellis gardening. *(Photo by author)*.

Eggplant grows in front of a trellis, squash at left; they are ready for training against the trellis rather than growing horizontally to interfere with other vegetables being grown. *(Photo by author).*

You will like blackberries much more if they climb a trellis rather than ramble through your yard. On trellises and in boxes they are confined and at the same time handsome, and of course good to eat. *(Photo by author).*

This fruit tree is being trained in espalier fashion against a trellis fence. This is an excellent way of growing fruit trees if you have little land. *(Photo by author)*.

Rambler roses on a charming simple trellis arbor frame a house entrance in color and beauty. *(Photo by Matthew Barr).*

4 Construction Data (materials)

Building trellises is relatively simple because in most cases you are working with lathing. Originally, lath was the thin wooden strip used in lath and plaster. Common outdoor lath was also used years ago for outdoor structures. Lath is redwood or cedar in dimensions of about ⅜ inch thick x 1⅝ inch wide. It is sold in lengths of 6, 8, and 10 feet in bundles of 50 pieces. Usually two grades of lath are milled: one grade has considerable knot holes and blemishes; the other grade is surfaced lath, almost but not totally free of imperfections. Use surface lath for your trellises.

Lath can also be made from 1 x 1 inch or 2 x 2 inch wood cut to size. When used in trellis or lattice patterns, lath is more commonly referred to as wood strips, of almost any type wood. These strips are much more expensive than standard lath and must be bought by the piece, not the bundle. The heavier strip is stronger and better looking than lath, and for projects like gazebos and arbors is better than laths.

Another type of strip used for trellises is batten *(as in the phrase board-and-batten)*. Battens are overgrown laths in thicknesses of ¼ to ¾ inch and widths of 1 to 2 inches. Battens can be purchased in lengths up to 20 feet and are sold either by the piece or by the bundle *(6 or 8 feet long and 30 pieces to the bundle)*. Battens are smooth surfaced and have substantially more strength than lath; they are recommended for more decorative trellises. Battens are about 20 percent more expensive than lath but not as costly as wood strips.

Which Wood to Use

The standard lath *(in bundles)* is quite satisfactory for most trellises in the yard or patio; it will last approximately 2 to 3 years. For more elaborate structures – fences, screens – use battens because they last for many years and always look good. For large structures like gazebos and archways, use the wooden strips. They look expensive, last years, and make a durable structure.

No matter which type of wood you decide to use, working with lath *(we will consider all three types of wood as lath)* offers a versatile way to make a number of outdoor structures, from the old-fashioned arbor to the more sophisticated pergola. Lath is inexpensive, easy to install *(a child can almost do it)*, and adaptable, so it can provide as much or as little cover as you desire while still providing a place for plants and decorative accent.

The most satisfactory lath wood is redwood or red cedar heartwood. These woods resist outdoor conditions because they contain decay-resistant oil and their straight grain makes them less liable to warp. Heat or cold, dry or wetness will not affect these woods if they are properly installed.

If neither of these woods is available you can use pine or fir, in which case you must apply some protective coating to protect them from the weather.

Other Woods

You can use tree branches for fashioning your own trellises and arches. This is not easy, but with creativity and perseverance you can make handsome hand-hewn structures. Any durable wood with some flexibility can be used; years ago, larch wood was used for arbor building. If you use tree branches, remove stems and twigs. Do not make your handmade trellises too complicated; stick to simple patterns. Fasten together larch poles or other woods with strong wire at interstices to nylon cord, hemp, or another natural fiber. Use basketweaving techniques.

Interlocking Lattice

Most trellises and lattices are constructed by nailing and epoxying a lath upon a lath in a cross pattern. If you are using heavier woods, nail one piece of wood on top of the other in a cross or diamond pattern or whatever. Generally, both these methods are fine for trellises, the latter of course being stronger than the simple lath on lath method. However, in some situations, where there is a great deal of wood or where abundant strength is needed to support plants, use the third way of building the trellis: the interlocking method. *(There is also a slight advantage in appearance with this kind of trellis.)* For the interlocking construction, follow these nine rules:

1. Use 1 x 1s, 2 x 2s, 2 x 4s.
2. Tape together bundles of 2- x 2-inch strips, ten pieces to a bundle, with the ends flush.
3. Mark across all pieces with parallel, 1-inch wide lines. Space the lines evenly.
4. Tape masking tape lengthwise on your saw to a 1-inch depth for 2-inch strips. Saw down as far as the tape, just inside your markings.
5. Take a small hammer and strike between the saw cuts to knock out the chunk of wood, leaving a socket or groove.
6. Insert 1- x 1-inch wood strips crossways into the grooves *(they should fit flush)*.
7. Use 2 x 4s for the frame.
8. Nail strips into grooved pieces.
9. Paint lattice or leave it natural.

Spacing Laths

The spacing of laths is important for three reasons: (1) to create a definite pattern, (2) to allow plants to have sufficient room to grasp wood, and (3) for shadow and light patterns. Generally, the following spacing data work well for all three aspects. For lath ½ inch in thickness or less, spacing should be ¾ inch. For lath ½ inch to 1 inch, use a ¾-inch space. For lath 2 x 2 inches, 1- to 2-inch spacing works well.

No matter what spacing is used, it must be constant throughout the overall pattern; any variations will be noticed, especially if the lath structure is used for decorative effect, that is, with little or no plants.

The "spacer" can be a wooden block inserted between the laths as you nail them in place. I use a block about 6 to 8 inches long. I lay it flat on top as I nail the lath in place and then again near the bottom when I nail the bottom of the lath in place.

Lumber Required

When you have figured the total area of the lattice work, the size of lath members, and the spacing, you can determine how much lumber you will need. As mentioned previously, lath is sold in bundles. Thick laths (1 x 1, 1 x 2, or 2 x 2) by the running foot. To determine how much lath to order, use this formula:

1. To determine the number of running feet of lath required per square foot of area: add the width of the lath and the space you plan to leave open between the lath, and divide the total into 12. For example: for 1½-inch lath spaced ½ inch apart, add 1½ and ½ and divide by 12. The answer is 6.

2. To find out how many running feet you need to cover an area, multiply the running

Cedar or redwood lath comes in bundles, here leaning against a trellis structure. Lath comes in 8 and 10 foot lengths and is relatively inexpensive. *(Photo by author).*

feet per square foot by the total number of square feet in the area: if there are 6 running feet of lath per square foot and 50 square feet to cover you need to order 300 running feet of lath.

For bundled lath you can determine the number of bundles to buy by figuring the number of running feet per bundle and dividing this into the number of running feet required. The number of running feet per bundle is found by multiplying the length of the lath times the number of laths in the bundle. Example: a bundle of 50 laths of 6-foot lengths would be 300 running feet.

Trellis structures must be heavy enough to support plants. For this reason substantial framing is absolutely necessary. Framing is suitable 2 x 4s on which to nail lathing. Rather than using very large or long frames, it is always better to makes smaller ones, say, a maximum of 4 feet long. The frame is usually 2 x 4s nailed together at the corners and further braced with L-shaped braces at each corner. Occasionally a brace – a piece of wood running across the frame – is used for additional support, but if this is done it must become part of the general design.

String and Wire Trellises

In trellis gardening you are not limited to wood; you can also erect wire trellises. These are cheaper than wood and perhaps not as aesthetic in appearance, but certainly serviceable and preferred for berry growing, for example. The general construction is almost the same as for wooden trellises. Put supports in place – usually 2 x 4 or 4 x 4 posts – and stretch wire across at top and bottom and then add two lengths of wire in between to make four wires. Staple the wires in place at each end of the posts. Leave more space between the wires than you would wooden trellises *(24 inches is good)*.

String trellises are sometimes used for vegetable growing since string costs little and ironically you can fashion rather handsome trellis designs with string. The basic support of posts as previously mentioned remain the same and string is usually wound around nails in the posts and stretched across to create desired patterns. The grid pattern as well as diamond patterns is easily created working with string.

Trellises You Buy

Commercially made trellises are already made up, in large and open-boxed, rectangular, square, fan-shaped, or canopy shaped designs. Commercial lattices or trellises are usually made of ⅛-inch stock and come in several heights, sizes, and qualities. These trellises can be used satisfactorily in the garden but usually are of flimsy construction and rarely last more than a few years.

Furthermore, their design is hardly pleasing, and you must work to the sizes available. Thus in most cases it is far wiser to build your own – the custom look cannot be surpassed.

Nails and Fasteners

Lathing nails, available at hardware stores, are flat-headed short nails. Use them to nail together one piece of lath over another piece of lath. Use regular galvanized-metal nails for the framing and attaching the frames to the posts. In addition to nailing, it is a good idea to use a wood epoxy when overlapping laths for additional strength.

If you make your trellises properly, you should never have to use wire to anchor them to other structures. But if you have gone amiss somewhere and need to use wire, buy the most unobtrusive but strong wire and camouflage it so it does not show. There is nothing tackier than a lovely well-made trellis wired to a support.

Once you have made the frames, attach them to something. Some people use an existing fence or whatever is handy, but ideally all trellises should be nailed to substantial posts. Four x 4 posts are usually the best. Sink the posts into concrete to a depth of 2 feet. Allow the concrete to set for a day or so; then put framing and lattice in place. If you build your structures following these principles, they will last years. In essence, trellis making for most structures is the same as basic fence construction: posts and stringers, and lattice rather than boards nailed in place.

Most lattices and trellises

are left to weather because redwood turns a lovely silver color after a year or so. However, sometimes the decorative effect is wanted; the trellis is painted. In this case, use 1-inch wood members because it is almost impossible to properly paint lathing to satisfaction. Even painting 1-inch stock is very difficult.

Patterns

There are dozens of patterns for trellises. What you pick depends on your own choice and the surrounding materials and space. Intricate designs – sunbursts, geometric – can certainly be used and will have dazzling eye appeal, but remember that the more intricate the design, the more time it takes to make the trellis.

If you decide on a special pattern for your trellis work, first make a sketch of what you want. From the sketch it will be easy to determine how much lumber you will need.

Grid This is the simplest, easiest to make pattern for trellis work and adapts well to almost any situation in the garden: on fences, against house walls, and so forth. Nail the lath at top and bottom, horizontally or vertically; then nail the other lath pieces on top at each end. The open work pattern allows air circulation and alternate sun and shade, which is good for all plants. Spacing for the grid pattern is usually 1 inch, but it can be closer if necessary.

Basketweave This looks like the grid, but the laths are alternated; that is, they are pushed under and over another lath to create a basketweave effect. The pattern is handsome but not always suitable for all plants because of the closeness of the lath. This is more a decorative trellis than a working one.

Framing is in place here and now lath is being nailed to the frame. Note the piece of wood used as a spacer before lath is nailed in place. *(Photo by author).*

Starburst The starburst design is a handsome pattern and it lends itself well to larger structures like entranceways, gazebos, and decorative archways. When you plan the starburst, never use too much; restrict the pattern to, say, the upper third of an entranceway or to the side panels, using more conventional up-and-down lathing to balance the structure. There are several starburst patterns – some horizontal, others vertical – so choose one that strikes your eye.

Diamond This is a variation of the grid pattern. There are diamond rather than rectangularly shaped openings between the lathing. Like the grid pattern, it is easy to make. Spacing is of utmost importance: keep spaces absolutely the same throughout the design. Nail laths in place at top and bottom, left to right; then nail the other lathing at top and bottom, from right to left, to form the handsome diamond pattern. Plants grow well on these trellises, and the diamond pattern is fine for fences, house walls, and even as accent panels throughout the patio or terrace.

Geometrical The geometrical pattern is difficult but not impossible to make. The design itself can be of several variations, depending on your own personal tastes (see drawings). Like the starburst, the geometrical pattern is dramatic and needs a large surface to be at its best. Thus it is ideal for gazebos and archways. Do not use this pattern for fences and house walls because it is just too powerful.

One-inch stock is used in this simple trellis; usually for decorative use 1/2 or 1-inch lumber is better than lath which is thin. *(Photo by Matthew Barr).*

46

This trellis is a commercial one found at most nurseries; it usually is not as strong as homemade trellises but is certainly satisfactory. *(Photo by Jerry Bagger).*

ARBOR TRELLIS

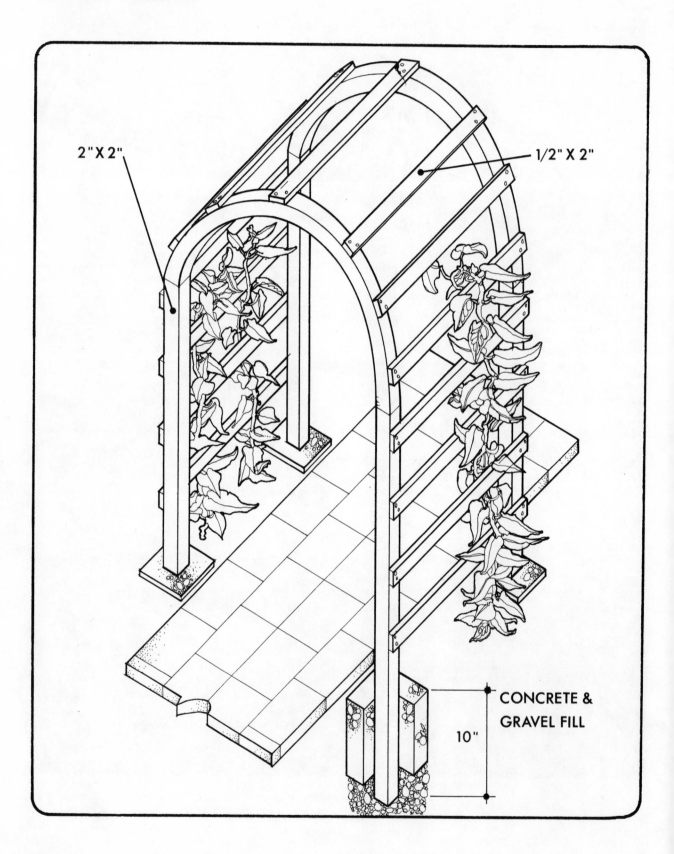

2" X 2"

1/2" X 2"

CONCRETE &
GRAVEL FILL

10"

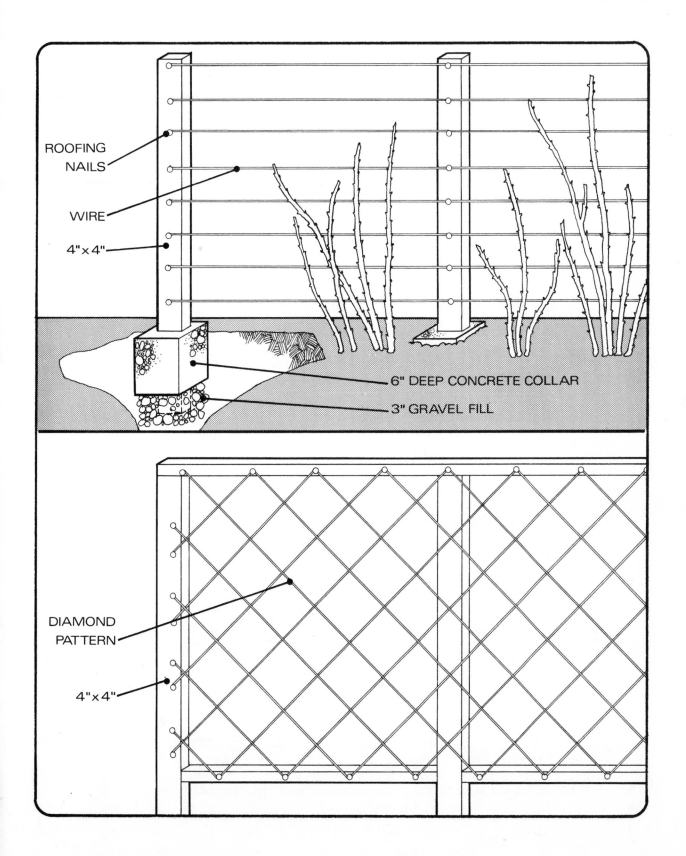

ROOFING
NAILS

WIRE

4" x 4"

6" DEEP CONCRETE COLLAR

3" GRAVEL FILL

DIAMOND
PATTERN

4" x 4"

STRING TRELLIS

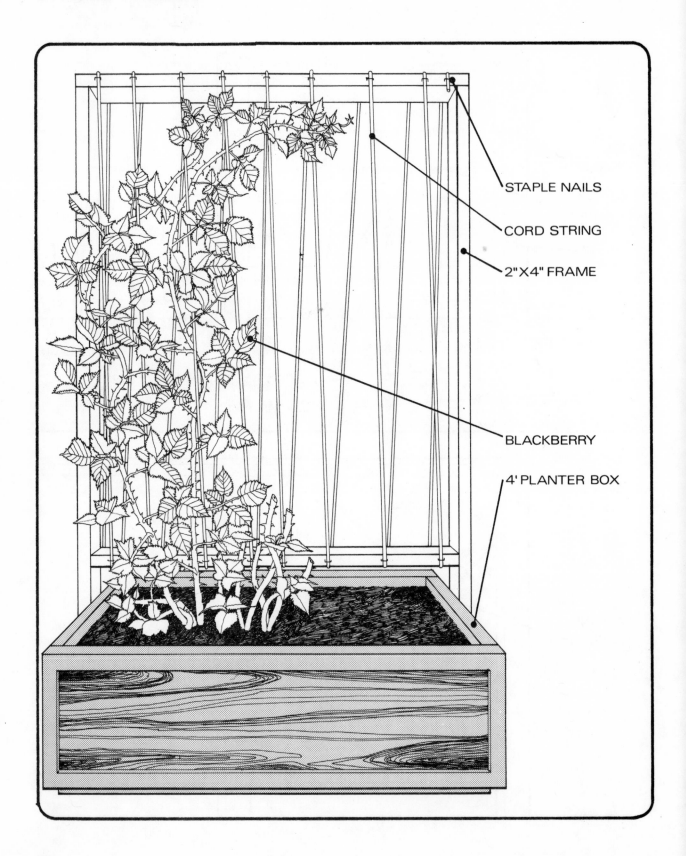

STAPLE NAILS

CORD STRING

2"X4" FRAME

BLACKBERRY

4' PLANTER BOX

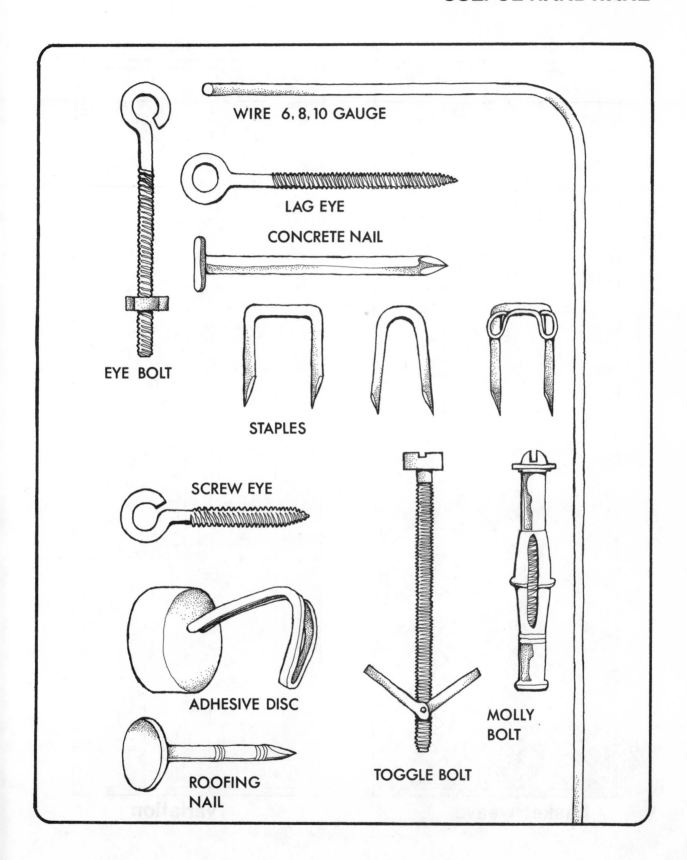

WIRE 6, 8, 10 GAUGE

LAG EYE

CONCRETE NAIL

EYE BOLT

STAPLES

SCREW EYE

ADHESIVE DISC

ROOFING
NAIL

TOGGLE BOLT

MOLLY
BOLT

TRELLIS PATTERNS

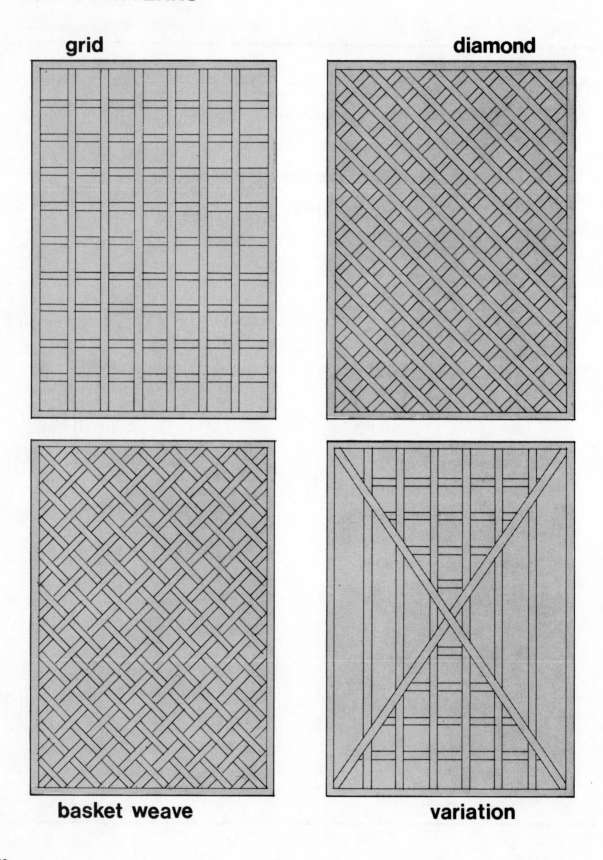

grid

diamond

basket weave

variation

Wire trellises can be used too (and should be for berry growing). Here the twining tendencies of morning glories are well shown. *(Photo by author).*

This is a very well-made ornamental lath trellis used as a barrier on a staircase and also for its decorative beauty. *(Photo by Matthew Barr).*

5 Containers

More and more container gardening is becoming popular, and rightly so because it is an easy way of growing plants if soil in your area is bad. Trellises adapt easily to containers; sink them into the soil in the pot. The container trellis garden can be anywhere: a porch, patio, deck, doorway, or balcony. Often commercially-made containers do not fit your space needs. Thus homemade containers are essential so you can accommodate the tiniest or the largest space.

(And making your own containers is cheaper than buying ready-made containers.)

If you are going to do trellis gardening in containers, just how you make the containers and what you make it of are vastly important. In this chapter we show and tell you how to build containers for many home areas. We also discuss the many commercially made containers so you will know how to choose a housing for your plants.

Containers You Buy

Many of the manufactured containers on the market are quite suitable for growing plants, but many are not. Size is the main consideration of a container; generally the biggest commercially made container – clay, plastic, or glazed ceramic – is 24 inches in diameter, tub-shaped. Also available and suitable for trellises are rectangularly shaped clay or wood planters. This type is very handsome but rather expensive.

Clay pots and planters are fine for most plants because clay allows moisture to readily escape; thus there is little danger of overwatering. Clay planters look well on decks and patios because they blend beautifully with the stone and other masonry material prevalent in these areas. In the garden, you can use clay containers or wooden ones which always suit the scene.

The one drawback of the rectangular clay planter is that it is so heavy when stationed in a specific spot that moving it is hard work. At present, 24 inches is the maximum length of the clay planter, but more sizes should be available in the near future. The square clay planter, about 18 by 18 inches, accommodates just one plant. Make sure any clay container you buy is deep enough to hold the plant you want to grow. For vegetables and fruit trees and vines, use a container with at least a 12- to 20-inch depth. And whatever the container's shape – box, rectangular, tub – be sure it has drainage holes.

Wooden planter boxes are at suppliers too and these may be of redwood or pine. While the designs of the boxes *(outside motif)* is not unpleasant, the boxes at present only come in three sizes: 16 inch, 24 inch and 30 inch lengths. If you can find the ones that have not been painted or stained red, they are attractive and can be used for your trellis gardening. Of course these boxes will not have the custom look that ones you make yourself have but if time is of the essence or if you simply are not handy with tools, this is one answer.

Rigid or flexible plastic containers are not as good looking as clay or wood planters. More important, soil in plastic containers remains moist for a long time, which can cause problems because waterlogged soil is harmful to plant roots.

Containers You Make

The advantage of the do-it-yourself planter is that you can make it to fit almost any area you have available. And a fitted box has a custom look that is usually more handsome than a purchased planter which may not exactly fit the specified area. All you need to fashion your own containers are a hammer, nails, and wood. Redwood is the best wood to use because it resists rot and looks good in most areas, harmonizing well with outdoor surroundings. Boxes can be made with 2 x 6s or 2 x 8s; for very large boxes, use 2 x 12s. A suitable size for most planters *(and one I have used for years with satisfaction)* is 2 feet wide by 4 feet long. Besides the rectangular- or square-shaped planter, you can also construct triangular or octagonal ones, depending on your needs and tastes.

Against fences and house walls the redwood homemade planter is a simple and inexpensive answer. You can use a single row of planters, but for a more pleasing arrangement and for more growing area in limited space, stairstep modular-type redwood boxes.

I have discussed here the basic wood planter for trellises – one that is easy to build in a few hours. However, planter box designs vary considerably and if you are handy with tools you can try notched boxes, sort of log-cabin wood type that slot together; this requires some skill with tools. Another type of planter that is strikingly handsome is the planter made with dowels and no nails. You might attempt this kind of container after you have mastered some of the others.

Again, if you have more time you can assemble the boxes or planters with screws and epoxies and forget nails. This is actually the best way to make wooden boxes because screws keep wood together without warping and epoxy will further add strength to the box. This again is a matter of time and how handy you are with carpentry.

Many people like to decorate the outside of boxes with designs – scored, grooved, or with lattice-work and this will add beauty to the planter. Indeed, there is an array of things you can do to the outside surfaces to further enhance their beauty.

Containers for Free

There has been a lot of talk about free containers such as bushel baskets and sawn-in-half wine casks and I suppose in times gone by these containers were free. Now, however, they cost money and it is a moot question whether they are worth the price.

Frankly, the bushel basket is only a temporary container; it eventually *(sometimes quickly deteriorates and the kegs and barrel halves just are not as good as they are said to be)*. Further they are difficult to get drainage holes into because wood is usually tough but if you want the decorative idea of wood kegs, and soy kegs, old pickle barrels and so forth, by all means use them.

Specialities

The "wood tree" and pyramid for trellis growing are becoming very popular, and they are easy to make. For the tree, just use 1 x 1-inch redwood 6 feet high and 2 feet wide. Make a grid, and place the grid in a wooden box. You can grow cucumbers, and tomatoes in the box and train the plants up the "tree" for an unusual trellis garden.

You can also make a pyramid by forming a triangle from three panels of 2-foot trellis. Place planter boxes at the bases of the panels. Plant vegetables and decorative vines in the three boxes, and train the plants up the pyramid. This design gives you three different growing areas.

Another arrangement is a window with lattice at each side. This provides a decorative effect and additional growing area. Place a 2-foot panel of trellis at each side of an 8-feet long windowbox. Nail 2 x 4 posts to the face of the windowbox and house eave to provide a frame for the trellises. The arrangement can be varied somewhat by using the trellis panels at each end of the window box.

The rectangular terra cotta containers in the forground are handsome and could be used for trellis gardening. *(Photo by Matthew Barr).*

Here some homemade containers are being constructed for trellis gardening. Note that the planters are elevated on small blocks of wood. *(Photo by author).*

Wooden planters such as this are sometimes available at nurseries but are more expensive than those you would make yourself.
(Photo by author).

This homemade planter of redwood is on a deck and supplies vertical growing space for vines. *(Photo by author).*

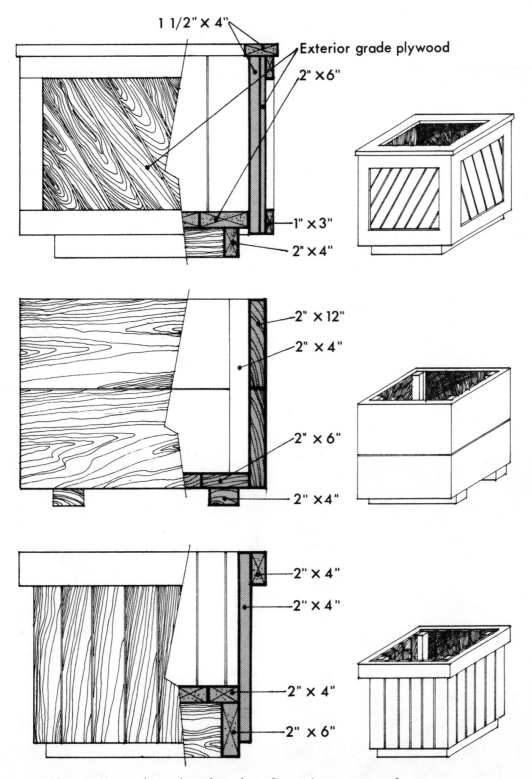

1 1/2" × 4"

Exterior grade plywood

2" × 6"

1" × 3"

2" × 4"

2" × 12"

2" × 4"

2" × 6"

2" × 4"

2" × 4"

2" × 4"

2" × 4"

2" × 6"

Lumber: pine, redwood, cedar; box dimensions: personal specs.

PLANTER BOX AND TRELLIS

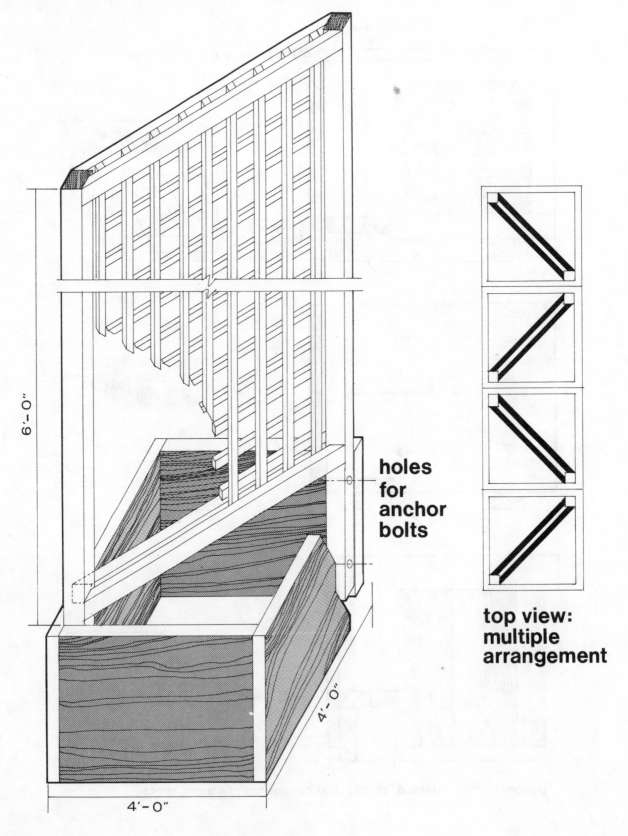

6'-0"

holes
for
anchor
bolts

4'-0"

4'-0"

top view:
multiple
arrangement

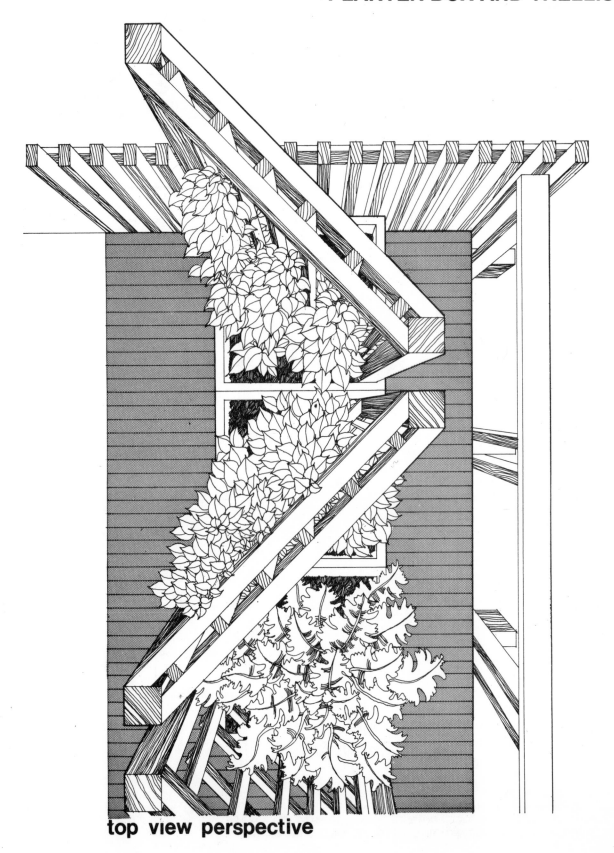

top view perspective

TRIANGULAR TRELLIS
TRIANGULAR TRELLIS

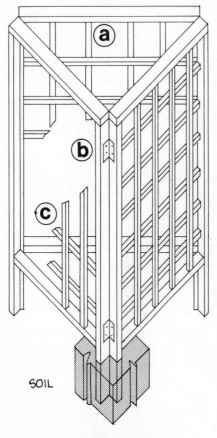

SOIL

FRAMING CONSTRUCTION

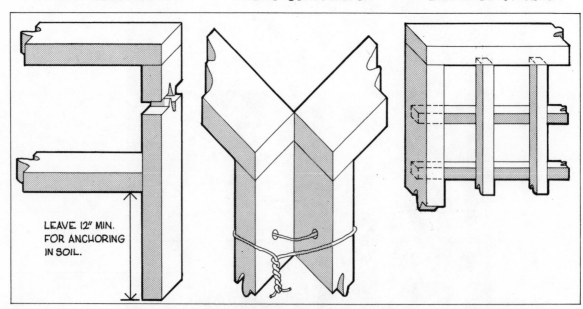

elevation

HINGING CONSTRUCTION

LATHING CONSTRUCTION

LEAVE 12" MIN.
FOR ANCHORING
IN SOIL.

(a) SIMPLE WALL-FRAME CON-
STRUCTION: TOP PLATE, BOTTOM
PLATE, WITH 12" MIN. FOR ANCHORING.

(b) MAY USE DOOR HINGES, OR AS
SHOWN ABOVE, DRILL HOLES
FOR TIE-WIRE ATTACHMENT.

(c) OVER-LAPPING LATHING
SPACED 6" APART. USE 3/4" X
3/4" REDWOOD STOCK.

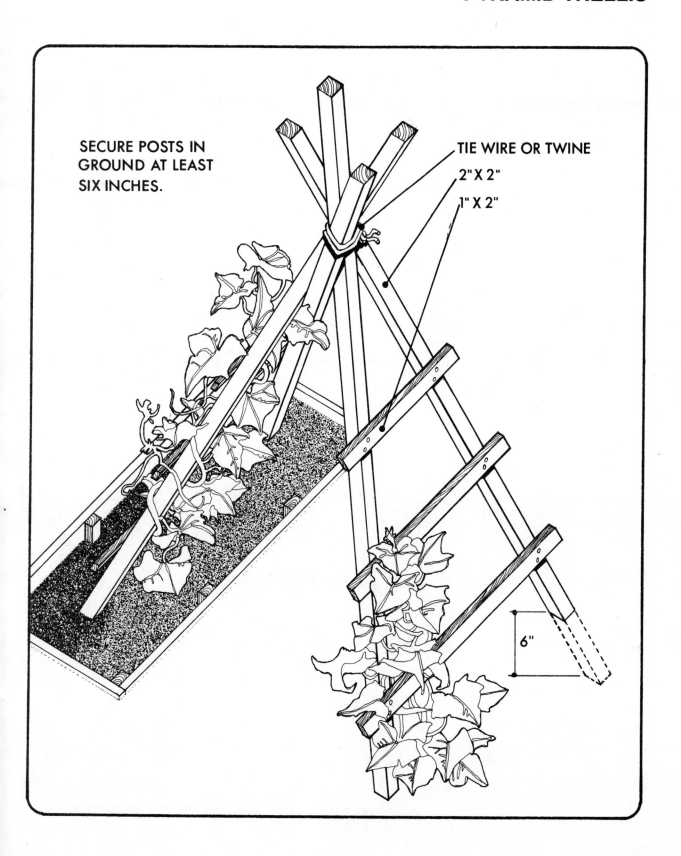

SECURE POSTS IN
GROUND AT LEAST
SIX INCHES.

TIE WIRE OR TWINE

2" X 2"

1" X 2"

6"

A teepee type trellis support is shown here for growing beans.
(Photo by Joyce R. Wilson).

6 Vegetables, Berries, and Grapes

My vegetable garden is, by necessity, in a tiny space (most of the grounds are ornamental gardens) so I save space and in the last few years have installed a trellis garden. So many vegetables – squash, pole beans, peas – are natural viners so I felt this would be an ideal way to grow them. What an improvement this was over standard garden growing! It was easier to reach and train plants and pick produce. Also, because plants were off the ground, insect problems were greatly eliminated. One final plus: my vegetables grown in trellis fashion looked much better, more compact; they had more eye appeal.

You cannot grow all vegetables on trellises, but squash, tomatoes, cucumber, peas, green peppers, bush pumpkins, and eggplant thrive when grown vertically. And with trellis growing you get double the yield you would from a 5- x 10-foot garden.

You can start vegetables from seeds, or buy prestarts available at seasonal times at nurseries. What you ultimately grow will depend on where you live, but there are varieties of vegetables for almost all areas of the country.

Planning the Vegetable Garden

You will not need a large plot of ground for trellis vegetable gardening. Even if you only have a walkway and fence you can grow some vegetables in planters *(wherever you can erect a trellis)*. If you do have space use the ground area for root crops like beets and carrots and as mentioned grow vining crops on trellises on fences or walls.

Do not try to do too much the first year; put in a few crops for trellis gardening and enjoy them rather than having so many vegetables that gardening becomes a chore.

You can grow vegetables directly in the ground parallel to fences or walls *(wherever you can erect a trellis)* or you can also use planters and put trellises in the planters for vegetable growing. Just what you do depends on the space and the character of the garden area. If you only have a patio it is far better to garden in containers but if there is a small garden area where you are growing other plants, then growing in the ground with trellis support may harmonize better with the overall scheme.

In your space saving trellis gardens you can grow many vining crops and these are the ones that are discussed here. The following list on vegetables will get you started and after the list you will find specifics about the individual vegetables.

Beans

Pole beans are an ideal crop for trellis gardening; they love to climb and a good harvest depends on tall lush plants. *(Don't confuse pole beans with snap bush type beans.)* Pole beans have more

Name	Planting Out Time Seeds	Seed Depth (inches)	Growing Days Needed	Remarks
Bean (pole)	After last frost	½-1	65	Excellent on trellis
Cucumber	After last frost	½	60	Do better on trellis than on ground
Eggplant	After last frost	¼	70-80	Bushy plants that will adapt to trellis
Peas	Six weeks before last frost	1½	60-70	May be grown on string trellis
Peppers	After last frost	¼	70	Start seeds indoors 8 weeks before planting out time
Pumpkin	After last frost	1	100	Where space is limited use bushtype 'Cinderella'
Squash (vine)	After last frost	1	Summer types 52; winter types 85-115	Many kinds. Check catalogs carefully for details.
Tomatoes	After last frost	½	70 from transplants	Sow seeds indoors 6 weeks before planting out date. Staked plants may be spaced closer than unstaked. Late crop tomatoes may be seeded directly in ground

flavor and are usually more productive than the bush beans. Dig deep generous holes for these vegetables and use a rich soil with some compost added to it. Fertilize beans with a vegetable food and grow with plenty of water. This is a warm season crop and seed should be planted about 1 inch deep.

Pole beans produce in about 60 to 70 days and can be picked at various stages of growth; the pods are usually ready about three weeks after blooms. If plants are healthy, you can pick beans every three to five days.

Peppers

Peppers are not true vining plants, but rather are bushy plants with dark green foliage and can be grown easily in containers with trellises or in the ground with trellises as supports, on fences or walls. Plants need a warm growing period of about 2 months, with night temperatures never below 65F. Start planting in April or May, depending upon your region.

There are long and slender hot peppers or the succulent sweet bell peppers. Peppers make attractive, bushy, 2- to 3-feet tall plants for patio, terrace, or porch decoration. Harvest your peppers about 8 to 9 weeks after the first transplanting. Frequent harvesting will encourage production through the summer.

Eggplant

A warm-weather crop, eggplant does best at about 80F during the day and 68F at night. Start seeds in April or May, depending upon your location, or buy prestarted plants. Eggplant needs a long and varm growing season; keep them ell watered and in a bright place.

Plants are easily trained to trellises and grow about 3 or 4 feet, depending upon the variety. Remove some blossoms as they appear so eggplant does not set too many fruits. Pinch back terminal stem growth to keep the plant bushy. Eggplant should bear in about 75 to 90 days; harvest immediately, even when the fruits are half size. If picked late, the fruit will have a bitter taste.

Cucumbers

Cucumbers are extremely robust, grow quickly, and these viners are ideal for trellis gardening. You can sow the seed directly in soil in a large 12-inch container or in the ground. Insert trellises so the plants can climb. Train the vine so the center becomes bushy and lateral stems develop sideways.

Give plants plenty of water, and be sure to add some manure to the soil. Keep plants in a bright place, although direct sun is not necessary. Cucumbers start bearing in about 40 to 70 days and can be picked at any stage. The young ones will be tiny but ideal for sweet pickles; larger ones, if you let them mature, are fine for salads.

Tomatoes

There are few things that beat the sweet luscious taste of freshly picked tomatoes. And tomatoes are perhaps the easiest vegetables for the neophyte gardener to grow. There are midget varieties specifically for container growing (they will still need a trellis) and standard varieties for soil planting. You can start your own plants from seed, but many people buy pre-started seedlings because there is a good selection available.

Tomatoes need warm temperatures and as much sun as possible to produce a good crop. Tomatoes are climbers so trellises are a good idea or they become a jungle; fasten plants to the wood members with tie-ons.

Give the plants plenty of water and good feeding with a tomato-type food (sold at nurseries). Keep the plants growing continuously so you have a good harvest. Fertilize first about a week after you transplant the seedlings and again in about 2 weeks. While plants are producing fruit, fertilize every week.

You can pollinate tomato blossoms by shaking the plant (assuming there are no bees in the area). New blossoms open daily over a long period of time. Keep tomatoes at temperatures above 60F at night or they may not set fruit. Very warm temperatures, over 95F, will also affect plants adversely, so shelter plants from extreme sun on very hot days.

Thin tomato plants by removing the small suckers as they form. These are the tiny first two or three leaves that appear between the main stem and the foliage. Depending upon the variety, tomatoes should bear within 70 to 80 days after seed planting.

Peas

Fresh garden peas are favorites of mine and this is an easy crop to grow. In spring as soon as the soil is dry, it is time to plant. You can also sow peas again in midsummer to have a second harvest in fall. Peas need a soil that has good porosity because they have long roots and they will need a support – the trellis works beautifully for them. If temperatures get too hot you will have all vines and no pods and don't forget to pick pods regularly; left on the vine too long they become hard. Plant seeds a dozen to a square foot of space, 1½ inches deep. Peas mature in about 60 to 70 days and while they are germinating they need plenty of water; later they do not need as much but still keep soil moist.

Watch out for aphids which cause stunted curly leaves on plants.

Pumpkin

I don't know just how utiliterian pumpkins are in the scheme of things but I do know they are fun to grow. The problem is you get too many pumpkins and actually all a family needs is one or two – for pie-making, for seeds.

The pumpkin, a vining plant, does well on trellises but be sure the wood supports are really strong to hold the weight of the plant. Use a good soil enriched with compost and select a sunny site for the pumpkin trellis garden. Direct seeding is best for pumpkins; plant seeds 18 to 24 inches apart and when vines start, thin them out so two strong ones remain and train these to the trellis. Provide plenty of water for pumpkins; plants need about 100 growing days for maturity.

I would hardly suggest pumpkins for the standard garden but for trellis gardens, they are fine indeed.

Squash

This is a natural vining plant that is ideally suited to trellis gardening. On the ground growing in conventional style squash takes up space and more space but on trellises it can be confined and still produce a bumper harvest. The plants are exceptionally pretty with large handsome leaves and huge yellow flowers and once started squash requires buckets of water *(and sun, of course)*. Feed every other watering and thin out plants to leave four or five stout stems for each 2-foot trellis. Pick vegetables early and often; they grow quickly and seem to double in size overnight and big squash invariably have little taste. There are summer squash varieties and winter types. *(Bush squash are also available but these would not be as good as the vining types for trellis gardens)*.

Squash borers can sometimes be a problem with this vegetable so dust plants with rotenone in July or August.

Tender Loving Care for Vegetables

To me, tender loving care means keeping plants healthy. If you follow only half the suggestions outlined here, the plants will grow. The real test of TLC is to keep plants free from the insects and diseases that can quickly mow down a garden. Like people, plants catch things from other plants, and once insects get a foothold they keep moving from one plant to the next.

Insects

Most common insect pests are discernible by the human eye; it is just a question of spotting

them. Aphids are tiny, oval, soft-bodied pests; mealybugs are cottony masses hard to miss; and scale are hard-shelled insects that attach themselves to plants and somewhat resemble apple seeds. All these insects are easy to see and easy to get rid of if you catch them early. The one insect you will not be able to see that is liable to attack plants is spider mite; you must hope that your plants are not attacked by this culprit. Dry air is a common cause of spider mite, so be forewarned.

In addition to the insects just mentioned, vegetables *(depending upon the kind)* will attract other unwanted visitors, although they may never appear if you keep a clean house. Chewing insects of various kinds love leafy vegetables, so keep rotenone insecticide on hand. Hookworms and cutworms may appear on tomatoes, but do not panic; hand pick and destroy them, or use Sevin *(only one or two applications is needed)*. Cucumber beetles are easily discouraged from squash and cucumbers by using a regular rotenone or pyrethrum insecticide. If you are growing beans, be on the alert for bean leaf beetles or Mexican bean beetles. Use Sevin.

Squash borers are nefarious critters, and I hate them because I love squash. These insects can wipe out a good crop; if you see them, dust with rotenone, especially in early July to August.

Last, but certainly not least, snails and slugs like vegetables almost as much as people do. Get snail and slug bait; Corys is the best if you can find it, but if not, try Buggeta. Sprinkle pel-

lets on the soil. Use these chemicals and all insecticides with care and only as detailed on the package. It is especially important in any type of vegetable garden to observe caution on labels about discontinuing use a certain length of time before harvest.

Diseases

Diseases rarely attack plants in a small garden. However, in the yard some of the common diseases such as blight, bacterial spot, and two serious tomato diseases – verticillium and fusarium – may attack, so have on hand necessary remedies *(available in packages at nurseries)*. But like insects that have favorite foods, diseases attack certain crops too. Many vegetable varieties are now disease-resistant; look for them because they are certainly worth the search.

Berries

Do not overlook berries for your garden no matter now little space you have. Berries are essentially ramblers and take up space, but you can grow them on trellises and keep them within bounds and still have a great crop of fruit to eat. Blueberries, blackberries, raspberries, and strawberries are delicious fresh from the garden. Berry growing on a trellis or arbor is a challenging adventure. It does take time to prune and trim and train, but the results are worth it, not only for eating but also for looks. Rambling berries on arbors and trellises have a lovely old-fashioned nostalgia that adds great charm to the garden. Berries are best grown on wire trellises; wood trellises with enough open space can be used too.

Select berry varieties that are suited for your geographical area. Blueberries are best in the cool northern areas; boysenberries and their relatives, blackberries and loganberries, are good in the humid south, and you can grow strawberries in almost any part of the country.

Care of berries is covered in the specific lists that follow.

Raspberries

There are several kinds of raspberries – red, black, purple, and yellow. Some are early producers, others yield crops in midseason and there are also late bearers. Select types best adapted to your area of the country *(ask your nurseryman or your local agricultural agent)*. Secure one-year old stock, virus-free.

Raspberries thrive on moisture and must have it to produce a bumper crop; they also need good drainage. Plant in early spring in northern sections; in fall in the south. Set raspberries 2 to 3 inches deeper than they were growing in the nursery and black and purple types one inch deeper. After planting, cut back red raspberries to 8 to 12 inches. Black and purple raspberries are cut back to ground level. Plants berries four to six feet apart with trellis supports running the length of the planting. With berries, wire is the best type of trellis; a span of 2 or 4 wires running parallel to the ground. Use post supports every 2 to 3 feet.

Red raspberries develop new shoots from both crown and root.

Canes grow vigorously in summer, initiate flower buds in fall, overwinter and then bear the following season. Once canes have borne fruit, they die back. The cycle will be repeated as new shoots appear to develop to provide fruiting canes.

The best procedure for raspberries is to allow five to eight fruiting canes per mature plant. Train these on the trellis. Once canes are established all you have to do is prune and thin them annually. Cut out old canes that have borne fruit and always get rid of unwanted suckers. Keep canes trained to the trellis with tie-ons or nylon string.

Black raspberries are grown similarly but not the same. They are less hardy than the red and must be planted in spring when weather is really settled. Space them five or six feet apart. When the shoots are two feet tall, start pruning; this will encourage lateral branching which will bear the following year. The laterals are trained to the trellis. By late summer or early fall fruit buds develop and during the winter will be dormant. In spring, laterals must be cut back to five or six fruit buds.

Problems

Raspberries have few pests and diseases and if you buy mosaic and leaf curl resistant varieties you will have little problems. Red spider may attack but it is easily eliminated with frequent hosings. White grubs can become pests but can be controlled with Malathion and rotenone will take care of any berry fruitworms.

Blackberries

Blackberries can be pests in the garden because they are so invasive, thus they are best grown in planter boxes. They can also grow rampant on trellises, but just prune them to prevent disorder. But for pure delightful eating, in jams, jellies, or plain, blackberries are so splendid that even if they need some care they are worth the trouble.

To keep blackberries from taking over, start them growing vertically on wire trellises. And since a well-grown blackberry can yield a lot of berries in a season, you do not need too many plants to assure good eating during the season. Blackberries have canes that will bear fruit the year after they sprout. When the canes die, new ones spring up to replace the old ones; thus an established plant can bear up to 10 years.

Blackberries grow best in milder climates and the south *(raspberries are best for cool moist regions)*. The blackberry is a shallow rooted plant that requires ample moisture and good drainage and protection from drying winds. Common blackberry varieties *(including thornless ones)* are hardy or semi-hardy or tender; pick the one that grows best in your area. Plant in spring in the north and in fall or early winter in the south.

When plants arrive, trim away long roots and cut back tops to about 6 inches. Dig deep holes, spread roots out fanwise, and fill in with drainage material and soil. Pack soil rather tightly around the collar of the plant, and leave 3 to 5 feet between the plants, depending on the variety. During the first spring and summer, keep suckers cut. As soon as young shoots are up 2 or 3 feet, snap off the tips so lateral growth will start to bear fruit the following year. Keep vines trained to the trellis using tie-ons or nylon string to keep them in place. The following spring, prune laterals to about 18 inches, and as soon as new canes are up, select four or five of the strongest and let them grow on the trellis. Remove others at ground level. When new canes are about 30 inches tall, tip them so they will prepare to bear fruit for the following year. Blackberries will bear some fruit in the second year, but the bumper crop comes in the third year.

Problems

Since blackberries are strong and vigorous plants, they are subject to few problems. Blackberry pests and diseases are likely to be the same as those for raspberries. *(See previous section.)*

Blueberries

Blueberries like an acid soil, so if you do grow them, be sure the soil has a pH of about 4.2 to 5.0. To make your soil acid, add peat moss or partially decayed oak leaves or acid food in packages. Do not add manure because it tends to make soil alkaline.

Blueberries are largely self-sterile, so you will have to have a few different varieties so plants will bear. The 'Highbush' variety does well in North Carolina, New Jersey, Massachusetts and Michigan, and grows to about 8 feet. The 'Lowbush' berry is a small plant, to 3 feet, and is fine for New England states. The 'Rabbiteye' is best for the southeastern United States and is a good plant because it adapts to many

soil conditions.

Plant blueberries when they are dormant, either spring or fall. Have trellises ready and space plants 6 to 8 feet apart, and prepare soil carefully with sandy loam, some sulfur, and sawdust. Dig large holes for each plant *(twice the size of the root ball)*, and set the plant high in the ground with the crown 2 inches above the soil level. Feed plants sparsely if at all because if fed too much, blueberries will be all leaves and no fruit.

Do not fertilize when planting bushes; wait until plants leaf out and are fully mature. Pinch of all blossoms the first year after initial planting. Unlike other berries, blueberries require little if any pruning. You can occasionally prune lightly, but what you want are tall erect strong canes. Keep them trained to the trellis structure. Prune just enough to encourage laterals or side shoots, which is where fruit is borne. Remove laterals after fruiting to make room for new shoots. After 5 or 6 years, cut away to the ground older branches that are not producing good laterals anymore. This pruning will continually renew the bush. Blueberries can literally bloom themselves to death, so it's up to you to keep them within reason by pruning off some laterals.

Problems

Blueberries are incredibly free of insects and disease if grown properly. Neglecting to pick fruit when ripe will encourage an entourage of fruit flies, so keep berries picked and clean up all trimmings promptly. If insects do attack, dust plants with rotenone. Birds love

blueberries as much as people do, so plant enough for everyone.

Strawberries

Strawberries are an amenable crop that even the beginner can grow. These plants, which can be cultivated in most parts of the United States, are perennials that live for several years, blossom, and bear fruit each season. The best crops are produced the first 2 years; after that, the yield is not great. Strawberries are usually called everbearing but there are really early, midseason, and late bearers.

Even a dozen plants will yield a harvest for the novice, sparse in the first year but prolific in the second year. When you are ready to start your plants, build a trellis pyramid for them. It takes up little space and looks good. Use three 3-foot trellises; tall supports are not necessary. Trim roots back to 4 or 5 inches, dig holes wide enough to accommodate the roots, and set plants in place. Set plants so that crowns are at ground level. If plants are too deep in the hole, growth will be retarded; if plants are too high, they will die. The plants need a rich moist soil and plenty of sun to do their best. The ideal soil is sandy loam, but even ir. lesser soils, if there is good drainage, strawberries prosper. In the north, start plants in spring; in the south, plant in the fall. Just how you space your plants depends on how they are grown since there are several ways of growing strawberries.

The strawberry plant is a member of the Rose family and has lovely white scented blossoms that resemble wild roses; leaves are produced on short woody stems. Train the leaves to the trellis securing them with tie-ons or string. Most gardeners pinch the first blossoms from strawberries to get a better yield: the strength of the plant will not be depleted by setting fruit too early, and the resultant crop will be heavy when the plant matures. I pinch off some, not all, of the blossoms and have a fine crop of berries. Not every strawberry flower produces fruit. Some blossoms do not have fruit, so cross pollination is necessary (done by insects or wind).

Problems

The best way not to have insects or disease bother your strawberry plants is to select virus-free plants at the start. But you still may have problems. The most damaging insect is the strawberry weevil. This sucking insect can ruin a crop. The crown borer is another pest. Suitable preventatives are at nurseries. Verticillium wilt and gray mold are the two most prevalant diseases that attack plants; these are carried by soil-borne fungi that infects the roots and kills the plant. Control for disease can be accomplished by using appropriate remedies (at nurseries). I cannot really recommend specific remedies or controls because I do not use them; my strawberries are rarely bothered by pests or diseases. Yours will not be either if you buy resistant varieties and virus-free plants.

Grapes

There are grape varieties suitable for growing in almost every section of the country. Just how you fare with grapes will differ from region to region. Some

people have little trouble; their grapes grow with abandon. But other gardeners are besieged with many grape diseases that injure their crops. Just what and where the difference is I do not know, but I know from my experiences that grapes are easy. I grow mine on trellises and arbors, make sure they have ample sun and excellent air circulation, and I never worry them to death. As a result, I get a good crop of grapes most but not all years.

Buy your grapes from local nurseries to get varieties that thrive in your area. Get them into the ground as soon as possible; plant grapes in early spring as soon as the soil is workable. Dig deep holes and spread out roots. Set the plant slightly deeper than it grew in the nursery. Now pack dirt tightly around the collar of the plants, but not too tightly; you want a firm support of soil.

There are several variations on starting plants, but generally this is the procedure. Prune the plants to a single stem and allow two leads to develop; shoots will grow from each of the buds left on the plant. Tie the most vigorous shoot to the trellis support as it becomes long enough, usually 4 to 5 feet. Space plants about 6 to 8 feet apart. Give some extra care to the young plants the first year. Well-decomposed manure is an excellent fertilizer to get the grapes off to a good start; put the manure around the plant but away from the stem by 3 feet or so. Fertilize only if necessary – not simply to fertilize. If plants are making good growth on their own, leave them be. Added fertilizer can harm them.

Grapes need lots of pruning; without it they will grow rampant and rarely give you a good crop. Prune grapes at planting time, taking off some roots and shoots. An annual pruning is essential to encourage vigorous canes to develop, to train fruiting canes, and to limit the number of buds on the vine.

You will often see vines started with one central trunk and four 1-year-old fruit canes – two on each side – growing on the trellis. This is a fine way to start the vines. After the coldest part of winter is over and before buds swell, a good pruning is in order.

In the third year grapes are considered mature vines. In early spring pruning is again necessary, to keep the vine to four lateral canes, each with six to twelve buds arising from the main trunk. Each bud will produce two to three clusters of grapes. Always leave two renewal spurs near the main trunk for the future fruiting canes and remove all other growth. The best canes for the lateral-growing fruiting canes are of medium size, about ¼ inch in diameter, straight, and unbranched. Train one cane each way on the trellis.

Grape Enemies

Grapes have their share of problems, depending on the climate and region. A small sucking insect called Phylloxera is perhaps the grape's worst pest. (Other pests include aphids and moths.) It is something like plant lice, either winger or wingless. One pest produces galls on leaves, the other feeds on roots. Adhere to the following schedule to avoid insect problems.

Spray Schedule for Grapes

When to Spray	Pest	*Materials to Use
Shoot growth is 8 to 12 inches long	Aphids Berry moth Black rot Leaf chewers	Malathion Carbaryl *(Sevin)* Captan
Just after blossoms fall	Aphids Berry moth Black rot Leaf chewers Mildew	Same as above
2 weeks after above blossoms fall	Same as above	Same as above
Berries touch each other in the cluster	Same as above	Same as above

*Use measurements and dosage according to directions on packages.

Grapes make natural trellis subjects and can be grown on wood or wire trellises. *(Photo by author).*

Cucumbers climb a trellis and trained against the support will be handsome. *(Photo by author)*.

Scarlet runner beans have already established themselves on this trellis and grow lushly. *(Photo by Jerry Bagger).*

Squash starts its life on a trellis; this one got too large and grew on the ground too long. It should have been trained to the trellis while young. *(Photo by author)*.

RASPBERRIES

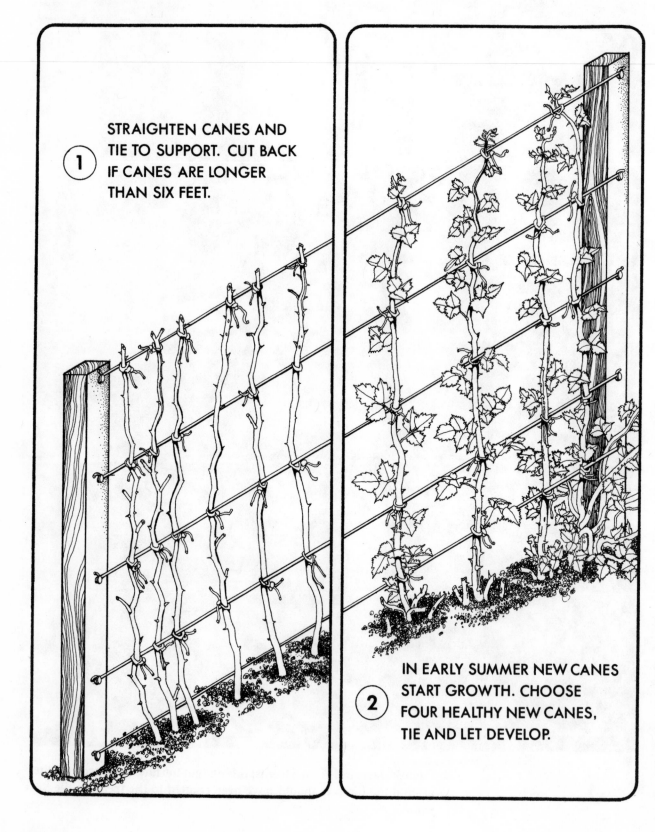

1. STRAIGHTEN CANES AND TIE TO SUPPORT. CUT BACK IF CANES ARE LONGER THAN SIX FEET.

2. IN EARLY SUMMER NEW CANES START GROWTH. CHOOSE FOUR HEALTHY NEW CANES, TIE AND LET DEVELOP.

BLACKBERRY

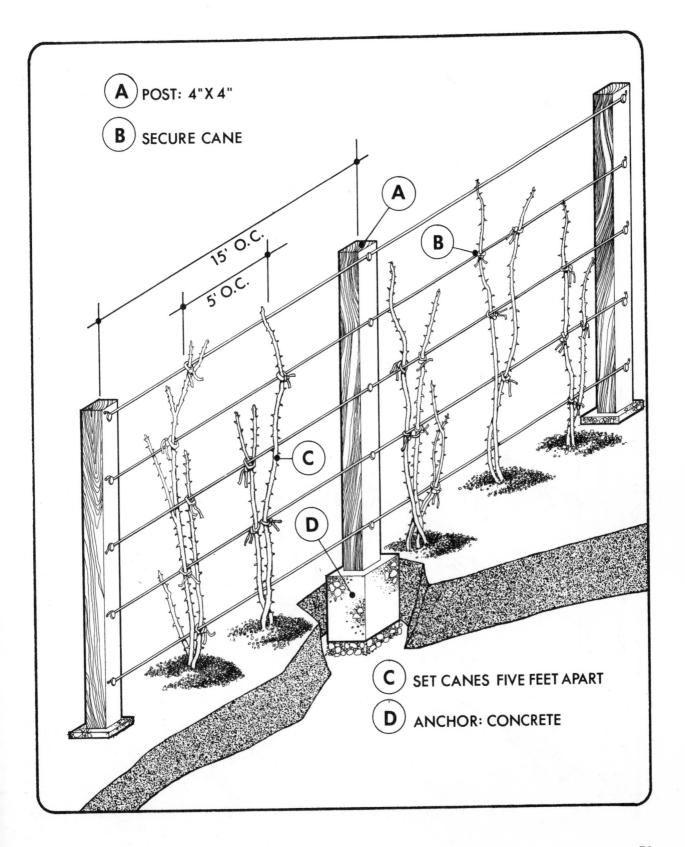

A POST: 4" X 4"

B SECURE CANE

15' O.C.

5' O.C.

A

B

C

D

C SET CANES FIVE FEET APART

D ANCHOR: CONCRETE

GRAPES

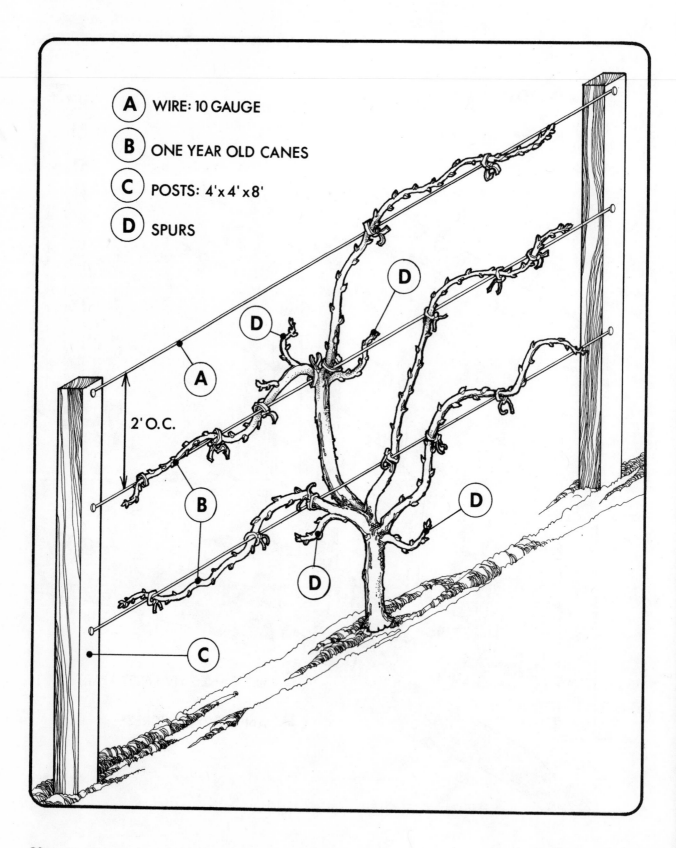

A WIRE: 10 GAUGE

B ONE YEAR OLD CANES

C POSTS: 4' x 4' x 8'

D SPURS

2' O.C.

7 Espalier/ Fruit Trees

Many people want to grow delicious fruits like apples and pears, but generally there is not space. What to do? Espalier the trees on trellises and have all and any of the fruit you want. For example, in a space of 20 feet, say against a fence, you can grow four dwarf fruit trees.

Training plants – all kinds of plants – to specific patterns is not new, but it is certainly an overlooked part of gardening. Yet a well-groomed espalier against a trellis can be more attractive than a row of foundation plantings, and think of the space saved!

Espaliering is working against a flat surface. A plant grown to an espalier pattern needs training and trimming to a desired shape. Generally, the plant is tied to a trellis that is parallel to a flat surface, with 4 to 6 inches of air space behind the plant. *(In some cases, espaliers are applied direcly to a wall.)*

If possible, buy *(at a nursery)* an espalier already started; it is much easier to train a tree or shrub that is already started than to initiate the pattern yourself. Do not be in a rush with espaliers; they take time to grow and cover an area, but once established, they are indeed handsome.

Espalier Patterns

Years ago there were rigid espalier patterns, but now the designs are personal choices. The formal patterns, although still seen, are not as popular as the informal or free-form espaliers. The formal patterns are quite symmetrical and include the following:

The double horizontal cordon. A center shoot about 20 inches high, with two horizontal branches in each direction.

The vertical U shape. A vertical stem on each side of a central trunk. Double and triple U shapes are also seen.

The palmette verrier. A handsome candelabra pattern.

The palmette oblique. Branches trained in a fan shape.

The horizontal T. A multiple horizontal cordon with several horizontals on each side of a vertical trunk.

Belgian espalier. A diamond pattern.

Arcure. A series of connecting arcs.

Informal espaliers are more natural and, to my eye, more pleasing for most properties. The patterns are casual or free-form. The informal espalier does not require as much trimming and training as the formal pattern, but creating an open and beautiful design is still the goal. Supports are generally not necessary; you can tie stems of plants to surfaces with special nails or copper wire.

Espalier fruit trees can be grown in containers or in the ground. Use a well-drained, rich soil, and choose appropriate plants for the conditions you can give them. For example, use sun lovers against a south wall, shade lovers at a north or west exposure. Do not fertilize espaliers; too much feeding will make it impossible to keep them trained to the desired shape.

Getting Started With Fruit Trees

Fruit trees bear at different times of the year. For example, there are apples for early season, midseason, and late season *(well into fall)*, so it is wise to select trees for the season you want. Just how long it will be before trees will bear is another consideration: apples and pears bear in 4 to 6 years; plums, cherries, and peaches bear in about 4 years.

Besides considering bearing season and length of bearing, you should also think of size. There are standard-sized fruit trees and dwarf ones that grow only a few feet. There are also many varieties *(kinds)* of apples, peaches, or cherries; your local nurseryman will tell you about these. Your nurseryman also stocks the type of trees that do best in your area, so ask for his advice. Your trees must be hardy enough to stand the coldest winter and the hottest summer in your vicinity.

Many varieties of fruit trees, including the tree fruits, are self-sterile, which means that they will not set a crop unless other blossoming plants are nearby to furnish pollen. Some fruit trees are self-pollinating or fruit-

ing and need no other tree. When you buy your fruit trees, ask about this. Fruit trees are beautiful just as decoration, but you do want fruits to eat too.

Buying Trees

Buy from local nurseries if possible, and look for 1 or 2-year-old trees. Stone fruits are usually 1 year old; apples and pears are generally about 2 years old at purchase time. Select stocky and branching trees rather than spindly and compact ones because espaliering requires a well-balanced tree.

Whether you buy from a local nursery or from a mail-order source *(and this is fine too)*, try to get the trees into the ground as quickly as possible. Leaving a young fruit tree laying around in hot sun can kill it. If for some reason you must delay the planting time, heel in the tree. This is temporary planting: dig a shallow trench wide enough to receive the roots, and set the plants on their sides and cover with soil and water them. Try to keep new trees out of blazing sun and high winds.

Planting Trees

Prepare the ground for the fruit trees with great care. Do not just dig a hole and put the tree in. Fruit trees do require some extra attention to get them going good. Work the soil a few weeks before planting. Turn it over and poke it. You want a friable workable soil with air in it, a porous soil. Dry sandy soil and hard clay soil simply will not do for fruit trees, so add organic matter to existing soil. This

organic matter can be compost *(Bought in tidy sacks)* or humus.

Plant trees about 10 to 15 feet apart in fall or spring when the land is warm. Then hope for good spring showers and sun to get the plants going. Dig deep holes for new fruit trees, deep enough to let you set the plant in place as deep as it stood in the nursery. *(Make sure you are planting trees in areas that get sun.)* Make the diameter of the hole wide enough to hold the roots without crowding. When you dig the hole, put the surface soil to one side, the subsoil on the other so that the richer top soil can be put back directly on the roots when you fill the hole. Pack the soil in place firmly but not tightly. Water plants thoroughly but do not feed. Instead, give the tree an application of B12 to help it recover from transplanting.

Place the trunk of the fruit tree about 12 to 18 inches from the base of the trellis; you need some soil space between the tree and the wood. Trellises may be against a fence or dividers or on a wall. Young trees need just a sparse pruning. Tie branches to the trellis with tie-ons or nylon string, not too tightly but firmly enough to keep the branch flat against the wood. As the tree grows, do more trimming and tieing to establish the espalier pattern you want.

To attach the trellis to a wall use wire or some of the many gadgets available at nurseries specifically for this purpose. For a masonry wall, rawl plugs may be placed in the mortared joints, and screw eyes inserted. You will need a carbide drill to make holes in masonry.

Keeping Trees Growing

Caring for fruit trees is not all that difficult. Like all plants, fruit trees need a good soil (already prepared), water, sun, and some protection against insects. When trees are actively growing, start feeding with fruit tree fertilizer (at nurseries). Use a weak solution; it is always best to give little rather than too much because too much fertilizer can harm trees.

Observe trees frequently when they are first in the ground because this is the time when trouble, if it starts, will start. If you see leaves that are yellow or wilted, something is awry. Yellow leaves indicate that the soil may not contain enough nutrients. The soil could lack iron, so add some iron chelate to it. Wilted leaves could mean that water is not reaching the roots or insects are at work.

Pruning

When a plant is dormant before new foliage has started in spring, do the heavy pruning. Or, on mature plants, wait until after flowering to start shaping them. With most plants, light pruning can be done every month during the growing season. Do not prune plants in late summer, as this would encourage new growth that would not have time to mature before cold weather.

Root pruning is not usually necessary with espaliers unless you have erred in choice, and the plant grows larger than you want it for a desired space. Do root pruning in early spring by spading out the ground 3 to 4 feet away from the base of the plant. This cuts off feeder roots and curtails rampant growth.

Fruit trees are subject to pests and disease occasionally. A dormant oil spray in early spring will discourage bugs. Ask your Agricultural Extension Service for information about diseases and what preventatives to use.

Apples

Apples can be grown in all the United States except Florida and is the hardiest of tree fruits. Apple trees can tolerate a wide variety of climates; some will even tolerate −20F. The ideal climate for apples is somewhat cool, with plenty of sun and abundant rainfall. Choose the variety that is best suited for your climate. Varieties that thrive in North Atlantic states may not grow in the South. Again, get the varieties most suited to your garden.

Apple trees can sometimes kill themselves by bearing too much fruit; trees should carry only as much fruit as they can support, so thin out fruit if you have the time. If the trees bear little or no fruit, the causes may be over production the previous year, a late frost that killed the flower buds, or lack of pollinization because only one variety was planted.

Pick apples when they are firm. Twist them from the tree; do not pull. If they do not come off easily with a slight turn of your wrist, they are not yet ready. If you pull off the fruit, the spur may come with it, preventing further fruit production.

Apple insects include aphids, leaf rollers, apple maggot, and scale; diseases are apple scab and blight.

Cherries

Cherries, sour or sweet, are an overlooked but delightful crop. The sweet cherries – 'Bing' and 'Queen Anne' – are delicious for out-of-hand eating; use the sour cherries for preserves, jams, and pies. Sour cherries are also much hardier and easier to grow than sweet ones. Generally, cherries grow under the same climatic conditions as apples. Sour cherries bear in the fourth or fifth year; sweet ones bear a few years later.

Make sure the cherry trees you buy are double bearing or pollination will be difficult. Cherry trees require good light, so be sure they are pruned properly every year: prune so that five or six limbs of your cherry tree become the main bearing limbs. Leave a single top growing straight up as a leader on the trellis but trim other branches so they are shorter than the leader. Prune so there is plenty of open space and good vertical shape.

Cherry trees are not as prone to diseases and insects (other than tent caterpillars) as most trees; they do attract birds that will eat the cherries long before you even see them. Ugly netting is one solution, but the best thing to do is pray and hope the birds arrive after the cherries develop or the cherries arrive before the birds find them. As a decoy, plant a mulberry tree; birds like mulberries even better than cherries.

Peaches

Peaches are a genuine taste treat, but peach trees try your patience. They will grow in almost all parts of the country, but they are temperamental, possibly bearing heavily one year but not the next. Peaches need both cold *(below 40F)* and warmth. Yet some varieties are very cold sensitive, so one cold snap can wipe them out. Yet without summer warmth fruit is sparse. But in spite of all their problems, peaches are worth every effort because they are immeasurably good and taste unlike any peach you will get at a market.

Buy the peach varieties that will tolerate your climate *(there are many peach varieties)*. Generally, peach trees are self-pollinating,

but it is wise to plant two or three trees. Trees will bear in about 4 years. Peaches need severe pruning when they are first planted because they do not take well to transplanting. By pruning the tops you encourage root development, providing the tree with a good start. Cut the leader *(center branch)* slightly; cut all other branches to about 4 inches. Tie stems to trellises with tie-ons or nylon cord to pattern desired. Prune slightly yearly; only initially give a severe pruning.

Peach trees are subject to some diseases such as leaf curl, but they generally are not bothered by insects to any great extent. One important cultural way to avoid problems with peaches is to keep the area around the trunk of the tree free of debris; otherwise bacterial diseases may start.

Pears

Pears need a good winter

chill to be at their best and will grow in the same regions as apples and peaches. Pears flower earlier than apple trees, so frost may be a problem. Unlike cherries and apples, which need a good rich soil, pears will do fairly well even in a poor soil if there is good drainage. Use different varieties of pear trees to ensure pollination (although they are mostly self-fertile). Pears need very little pruning, almost none, so do not worry about them as you would with apples or peaches.

At the start tie branches to the trellis, cut away errant branches and leaves, and train to desired espalier pattern. Pears do exceptionally well as espalier subjects.

Fire blight, the nemesis of pear trees, can strike all parts of the tree; symptoms are scorched areas. Trim any blighted area as soon as you see it. Do not wait. The worst time for blight is from bloom to fruit, so keep close observation during this period.

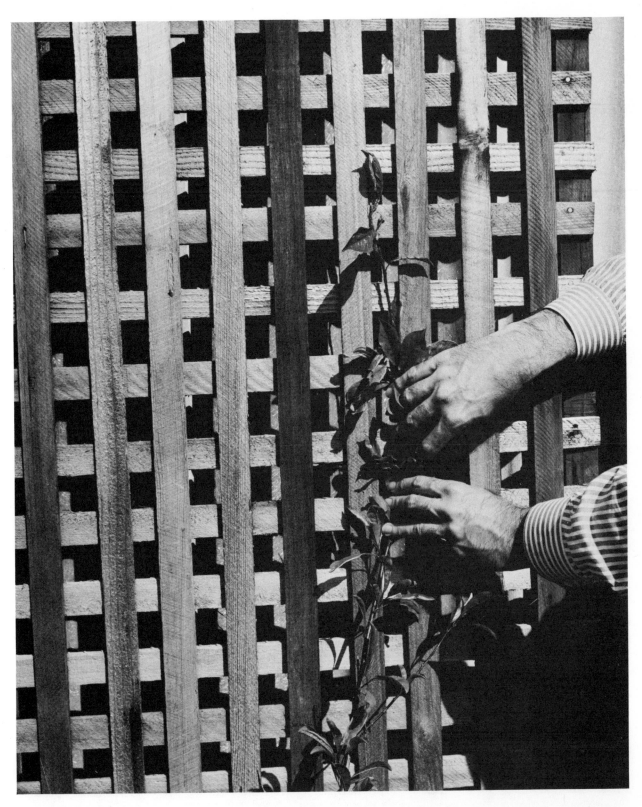

This photo shows how to start a young fruit tree against a trellis for espalier growing. *(Photo by author).*

Pear trees against a wire trellis. *(Photo by author).*

This handsome patio uses espaliered plants as the accent of the area; it is an impressive sight. *(Photo courtesy National Concrete Association).*

The trellis for this plant is too small and the plant has not been properly trained in espalier fashion. Avoid such use of trellis-and-plant work. *(Photo by Joyce R. Wilson).*

8 Decorative Vines

Vines, an essential part of any good landscape plan, are "naturals" for trellises. They screen walls or fences or block out an objectionable view. Vines fit into small spaces, can assume many shapes, and are breathtaking in bloom. Vine-covered trellises are especially suitable for rustic-type houses because the vertical lacy greenery makes the house look "grander" than it is and adds a great deal of decorative value to the total property. If used with discretion, vine-covered trellises add elegance to the traditional house and site; this is natural beauty on a grand magnitude.

Most vines, however, require constant pruning and attention because many vines are rampant growers that can take over an area. But there are many other vines that stay within bounds with little care. Some of the climbing vines, for example, clematis, bougainvil-lea, and morning glory, can, with proper care, become delightful screens of living color. Vines such as stephanotis, and some jasmines have a dainty and fragile quality, which is often necessary to soften harsh garden walls and house lines. And many vines – euonymus, and pyracantha – have colorful winter berries that are indispensable in the snow landscape.

Some vines, like jasmine, climb by means of twining or arching stems that need support; other vines have tendrils, disks, or leaflike appendages which grasp the trellis.

Besides differing as to growth habit, vines vary in appearance: some may be open and delicate, and others are heavy, with masses of foliage. Several varieties grow rapidly in a few months, but others take years to fill a space. Select vines carefully, not indiscriminately, or constant care will be needed.

Care of Vines

Plant woody vines in a hole 3 to 4 feet deep so the roots have ample space to grow. Replace the dug-out soil with good topsoil, but do not use manure or fertilizers because they may burn the plants. When the plant is in place, gently tamp the earth around the collar of the plant so air pockets will not form. Water thoroughly and deeply, tie stems to trellises, and for the first few weeks watch the plant to see that it is getting started. Once established, give the plant routine care.

Put vines in the ground at the same level at which they were growing in the nursery, and by all means try not to disturb the roots. Keep the root ball intact. If roots are disturbed, the vine will need more time to adjust to its new condition. Prune, thin, and shape vines at regular intervals to keep them looking handsome.

General list of vines

Botanical and Common Name	Minimum Night Temp., °F	General Description	Sun or Shade	Remarks
Akebia quinata (*five-leaf akebia*)	−20 to −10	Vigorous twiner; fragrant, small flowers	Sun or partial shade	Needs strong trellis; prune in fall/ early spring
Allamanda cathartica	Tender	Dense, with heavy stems; lovely tubular flowers	Sun	Prune annually in spring
Ampelopsis brevipedunculata (*porcelain ampelopsis*) (*blueberry climber*)	−20 to −10	Strong grower with dense leaves	Sun or shade	Prune in early spring
Antigonon leptopus (*coral vine*)	Tender	Excellent as screen	Sun	Needs light trellis; prune hard after bloom
Aristolochia durior (*Dutchman's pipe*)	−20 to −10	Big twiner with mammoth leaves	Sun or shade	Needs sturdy trellis; prune in spring or summer
Bignonia capreolata (*Clytosoma*) (*cross vine*), (*trumpet vine*)	−5 to 5	Orange flowers	Sun or shade	Thin out weak branches in spring; clings by disks
Celastrus scandens (*American bittersweet*)	−50 to −35	Light green leaves, red berries	Sun or shade	Prune in early spring before growth starts
Clematis armandii (*evergreen clematis*)	5 to 10	Lovely flowers and foliage; many colors	Sun	Needs strong trellis; prune lightly after bloom
Euonymus fortunei (*wintercreeper*)	−35 to −20	Shiny leathery leaves; orange berries in fall	Sun or shade	Needs strong trellis; prune in early spring
Fatshedera lizei	20 to 30	Grown for its handsome foliage	Shade	No pruning needed
Ficus pumila (*repens*) (*creeping fig*)	20 to 30	Small heart-shaped leaves	Partial shade	Thin plant in late fall or early spring
Gelsemium sempervirens (*Carolina yellow jessamine*)	Tender	Fragrant yellow flowers	Sun or partial shade	Needs strong trellis; thin plant immediately after bloom
Hedera helix (*English ivy*)	−10 to −5	Scalloped leaves; many varieties	Shade	Prune and thin in early spring

General list of vines

Botanical and Common Name	Minimum Night Temp., °F	General Description	Sun or Shade	Remarks
Hydrangea petiolaris (*climbing hydrangea*)	−20 to −10	Heads of snowy flowers	Sun or partial shade	Thin and prune in winter or early spring
Ipomoea purpurea (*morning glory*)	Tender	White, blue, purple, pink, or red flowers	Sun	Bloom until frost
Jasminum nudiflorum	−10 to −5	Yellow flowers	Sun or shade	Needs strong trellis; thin and shape annually after bloom
J. officinale (*white jasmine*)	5 to 10	Showy dark green leaves and white white flowers	Sun or shade	Provide strong trellis; thin and shape after bloom
Kadsura japonica (*scarlet kadsura*)	5 to 10	Bright red berries in fall	Sun	Needs strong trellis; prune annually in early spring
Lonicera caprifolium (*sweet honeysuckle*)	−10 to −5	White or yellow trumpet-shaped flowers	Sun	Prune in fall or spring
L. japonica 'Halliana' (*Hall's honeysuckle*)	−20 to −10	Deep green leaves that turn bronze in fall	Sun or shade	Provide strong trellis; prune annually in fall and spring
L. hildebrandtiana (*Burmese honeysuckle*)	20 to 30	Shiny dark green leaves	Sun or partial shade	Needs strong trellis; prune in late fall
Mandevilla suaveolens (*Chilean jasmine*)	20 to 30	Heart-shaped leaves and flowers	Sun	Trim and cut back lightly in fall; remove seed pods as they form
Parthenocissus quinquefolia (*Virginia creeper*)	−35 to −20	Scarlet leaves in fall	Sun or shade	Prune in early spring
Passiflora caerulea (*passion flower*)	5 to 10	Spectacular flowers	Sun	Needs strong trellis; prune hard annually in fall or early in spring

General list of vines

Botanical and Common Name	Minimum Night Temp., °F	General Description	Sun or Shade	Remarks
Phaseolus coccineus *(scarlet runner bean)*	Tender	Bright red flowers	Sun	Renew each spring
Plumbago capensis *(plumbago)*	20 to 30	Blue flowers	Sun	Prune somewhat in spring
Pueraria thunbergiana *(Kudzu vine)*	−5 to 5	Purple flowers	Sun or partial shade	Provide sturdy trellis; cut back hard annually in fall
Rosa *(rambler rose)*	−10 to −5	Many varieties	Sun	Need trellis; prune out dead wood, shorten long shoots, and cut laterals back to 2 nodes in spring or early summer after bloom
Vitis coignetiae *(glory grape)*	−10 to 5	Colorful autumn leaves	Sun or partial shade	Needs sturdy trellis; prune annually in fall or spring
Wisteria floribunda *(Japanese wisteria)*	−20 to −10	Violet-blue flowers	Sun	Provide overhead trellis; and prune annually once mature to shorten long branches after bloom or in winter; pinch back branches first year

Almost any vine is at its best on trellises and here morning glories are resplendent in color and form. *(Photo by Jerry Bagger).*

Jasmine tops this pergola with a cascade of beauty; a handsome addition to any garden. *(Photo by author).*

Rambling roses are colorful on this arbor and effectively frame the small garden. *(Photo by Jerry Bagger).*

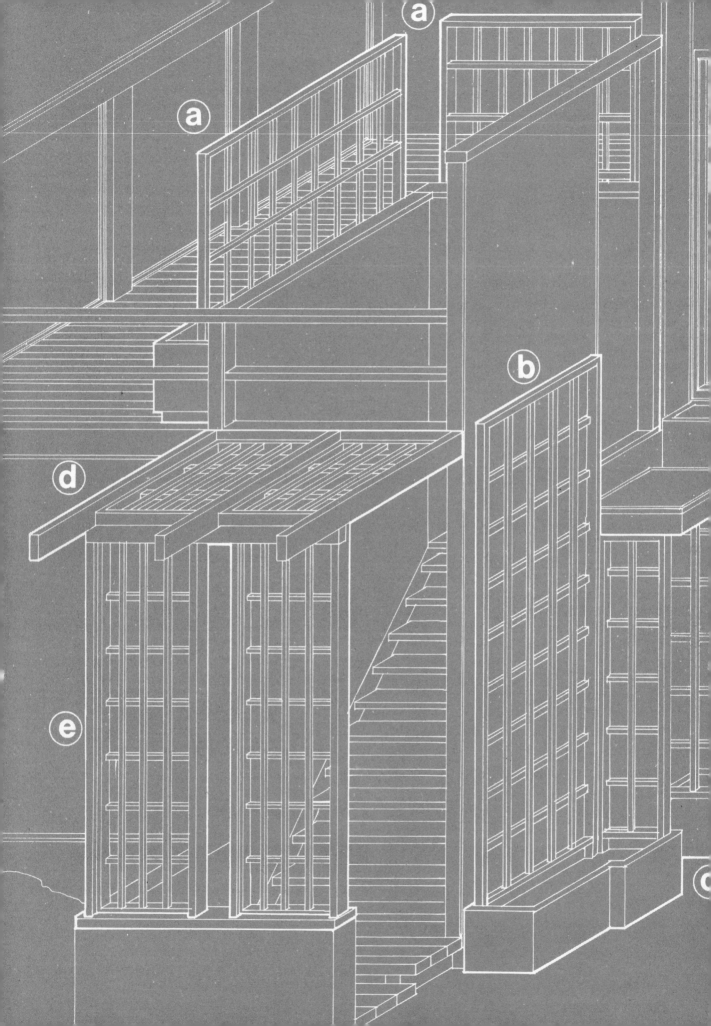